*Fundamentals of
Quality Auditing*

Also available from ASQC Quality Press

Quality Audits for Improved Performance, Second Edition
Dennis R. Arter

The Quality Audit: A Management Evaluation Tool
Charles A. Mills

The ISO 9000 Auditor's Companion
Kent A. Keeney with Joseph J. Tsiakals

The Audit Kit
Kent A. Keeney

Quality Management Benchmark Assessment, Second Edition
J. P. Russell

Audit Standards: A Comparative Analysis, Second Edition
Walter Willborn

Standard Manual of Quality Auditing: A Step-by-Step Workbook with Procedures and Checklists
Greg Hutchins

How to Plan an Audit
ASQC Quality Audit Technical Committee; Charles B. Robinson, editor

How to Make the Most of Every Audit: An Etiquette Handbook for Auditing
Charles B. Robinson

To request a complimentary catalog of publications, call 1-800-248-1946.

Fundamentals of Quality Auditing

B. Scott Parsowith

ASQC Quality Press
Milwaukee, Wisconsin

Fundamentals of Quality Auditing
B. Scott Parsowith

Library of Congress Cataloging-in-Publication Data

Parsowith, B. Scott, 1953–
      Fundamentals of quality auditing / B. Scott Parsowith,
         p.   cm.
      Includes bibliographical references and index.
      ISBN 0-87389-240-2 (alk. paper)
      1. Quality control—Auditing. I. Title.
TS156.P293 1995
658.5'62—dc20   95-15802
                                                                      CIP

10 9 8 7 6 5 4 3 2 1

ISBN 0-87389-240-2

Acquisitions Editor: Susan Westergard
Project Editor: Jeanne W. Bohn

ASQC Mission: To facilitate continuous improvement and increase customer satisfaction by identifying, communicating, and promoting the use of quality principles, concepts, and technologies; and thereby be recognized throughout the world as the leading authority on, and champion for, quality.

For a free copy of the ASQC Quality Press Publications Catalog, including ASQC membership information, call 800-248-1946.

Printed in the United States of America

 Printed on acid-free recycled paper

 ASQC
Quality Press
611 East Wisconsin Avenue
Milwaukee, Wisconsin 53202

*To the memory of my parents, Marty and Pearl,
and to my family: Sandy, Roni, and Pam*

Contents

Preface

Achieving excellence—*quality*—is a primary goal of businesses and companies around the world. In order to achieve this goal, individuals need to understand how to evaluate quality systems and use auditing as a management tool for fostering ongoing improvement. They also must become familiar with the quality systems and auditing standards used nationally and internationally.

As we move into the next decade, the quality of products and services will be defined by superior quality systems and the effective use of process controls. Quality auditing is one method of evaluating the documentation, implementation, and effectiveness of these quality systems. Hence the need for a book that gives a fundamental understanding of what constitutes a total quality system and the necessary ingredients for developing a successful auditing program.

Although it is generally recognized that internal and external auditors must maintain their objectivity and independence from the operation being audited, I believe that the true value of quality auditing lies in changing the focus from imposing corrective actions resulting from an audit to training employees in the use of quality auditing. Employees can then look to enhance quality within their own units through self-assessments. They can present issues of concern regarding processes and procedures to management for correction, rather than relying on independent management reviews that issue orders for corrective action due to findings of an audit.

I recommend that this practice be adopted by all companies, in order to shift the burden from the individual auditor to the employees who would use continuous "mini-self-assessments" of their units to ensure compliance to policies, contracts, and process requirements, as part of the continuous quality improvement effort. Implementing this practice would also reduce the tension and adversarial attitude between auditor and auditee that exists during the present system of auditing.

In the interest of achieving these goals, this book helps train all employees in the quality auditing function. This book provides an overall view of total quality management (TQM) in terms of the quality auditing function, which can then be incorporated into the everyday aspects of a company's operations and continuous quality improvement process.

Chapters 1 and 2 introduce the concepts of quality auditing, define the terminology, and provide applications for their usage. Chapters 3, 4, and 5 deal with the phases of the auditing process: initiation, preparation, performance, reporting, and closure. Chapter 6 provides guidelines for the setup and administration of a quality auditing program. Although it is primarily geared toward the establishment of an internal quality auditing program, its components may be used to develop an external quality auditing program as well.

Chapters 7, 8, and 9 describe the elements that can be used as a guide for a utopian total quality system. If auditors are to correctly evaluate a quality system, they should become familiar with the elements that form the system and be able to assess the implementation of them. The elements of this utopian quality system incorporate the most prominent features of nationally and internationally recognized standards such as the ANSI/ISO/ASQC 9000 Standards, which are the American version of the ISO 9000 standards, the MIL-Q-9858A, and the nuclear specification IO CFR, part 50, appendix B.

I have included quality costs as an element of a total quality system, as many companies use quality costs and standard costs to evaluate where opportunities for continuous improvement and product costs reside. Chapter 9, Element 21, defines a quality cost system. Appendix B further elaborates on the categorization of quality costs.

Chapter 10 is a brief summary of statistical process control (SPC) techniques used by many companies as part of their continuing quality improvement effort. This chapter is included to familiarize readers with these techniques so that quality auditors can evaluate whether statistical techniques are being properly applied by the company being audited. For easy reference, Appendix A has been included to provide the auditor with basic formulas used in the generation of control charts.

Chapter 11 provides a guide of simple sampling plans that quality auditors may use to assess a particular quality element, process, or product. Although there are many books that provide elaborate and extensive sampling techniques and sampling plans, this book provides a hands-on application of two simple sampling methods particular to the quality auditing field: estimation sampling and discovery sampling.

Appendices D and E provide easy-to-read tables to determine the number of samples to be taken at a particular confidence level and nonconformance rate. These tables include a wide range of field sizes in an attempt to cover the majority of situations quality auditors might experience. Appendix D contains the tables for estimation sampling—

attributes. Appendix E contains the tables for discovery sampling. Appendix C provides a random number table for the unbiased selection of samples.

The original idea of writing this book came as a result of the need for a training course by the Harrisburg Chapter of the American Society for Quality Control (ASQC) for employees/companies who wanted to be better versed in quality auditing and take the Certified Quality Auditor (CQA) exam given by ASQC. At the time, I was teaching quality management for the Continuous Education Program at Penn State York campus. The director of training for the Continuing Education Program at Penn State felt that a quality auditing certificate program should be developed to meet the needs of the business community.

This course was so well-received, I felt it should be formalized into a book. This book is a composite of many established authorities in the auditing field and provides the reader with the fundamental concepts of quality auditing principles. Transparency masters to be used in conjunction with the narrative in this book can be purchased separately as a tool for instructing the quality auditing process. In addition, the transparency masters provide instructors with a method for teaching students the various aspects of quality auditing. I recommend that the books and authors listed in the Bibliography be sought out for additional reading.

This book is based on my many years of experience in the quality management and quality auditing field. I have tried to provide an easy reference for the worker in the field in order to implement auditing techniques. I also believe the time has come for a book on auditing that includes some serious treatment of sampling and general statistics.

The intent of this book is to dissect and explain the quality auditing process so quality audits aren't viewed as something painful that is done to the auditee by someone else. This book presents quality auditing as a means of improving the quality system, with emphasis on the use of mini-self-assessments and how they can be fundamentally beneficial in providing feedback for continuous improvement. To achieve this goal, I recommend that all associates of a company use this book.

In addition, this book may also be used as a training tool for college courses in quality auditing, consultants in the auditing field, companies establishing and implementing the quality auditing functions in their organizations, and those planning to take the ASQC CQA exam.

Acknowledgments

This book has benefitted from the help of many people who have contributed their time and expertise to making this a better piece of work.

For his assistance with Chapter 10, "Statistical Process Control," many thanks to John S. Nelson of Pennsylvania Steel Technologies, Steelton, Pennsylvania.

I am grateful to the following people for their encouragement, advice, and revisions to various chapters contained within the book: Bernie Carpenter, Jim Dolan, Ed Hildebrand, Vince Gentilcore, Pete Jacoby, David Laudenslager, and Dave Wirick.

I would also like to acknowledge my fellow employees at Bethlehem Steel Corporation for the writing and implementation of the Bethlehem Steel Supplier Excellence and Auditor Training Program. This formed the nucleus for the development of my auditing course, which led to writing this book.

I especially wish to thank Kirk Gibson of Pennsylvania Steel Technologies, grammarian extraordinaire, for his enthusiastic attention to detail in reviewing this book.

I am also grateful to Colleen Taylor, who typed and retyped page after page during the many revisions and rewritings of this book.

Last, but not least, I am deeply indebted to my dear wife, Sandy, for her editorial and secretarial expertise along with the support and encouragement I received from her during the endless days, nights, and weekends it took to complete this book. And to my two dear daughters, Roni and Pam, I thank you for giving up part of our family life so that this book could be written.

Chapter 1

Overview of Quality Auditing

Auditing is both an art and a science. A basic knowledge of quality systems and specifications, although necessary, is not always enough. A good quality auditor also possesses an instinct for investigating, analyzing, and communicating. An auditor must be trained in quality functions, procedures, and principles; investigative techniques; and data collection techniques and must have hands-on job experience. This chapter will provide an introduction to the aspects of quality auditing.

Auditing should not be seen as a dreaded adversarial experience. Rather, it should be considered part of the continuous quality improvement effort used to improve the quality of the product or service, both internally and externally.

As an auditor, it is important to be attuned to your surroundings and to be able, based upon your observations and investigations, to assess the quality system of the company being audited. The auditor's function is to investigate, verify, and confirm. Using proper questioning techniques and asking the right questions is necessary to get to the root cause of why things happen. Therefore, communication is an essential tool for the auditor.

Communication is not easy because something said doesn't mean it was said correctly; something said correctly doesn't mean it has been heard; something heard doesn't mean it was understood; something understood doesn't mean it has been agreed upon; something agreed upon doesn't mean it has been applied; something applied doesn't mean it has been continually practiced. Verifying audit observations with fellow team members is vital. This allows for the identification and analysis of similar audit observations that occur in different areas of the same quality system.

In order to determine if the auditee has implemented the required quality criteria in its quality program, an evaluation must be performed on a sample of the criteria comprising its quality system. Sample size must be considered. There is risk in having too small an amount of samples. In chapter 11, proper sampling techniques will be discussed.

In general, there are three different types of audits: system audit, process audit, and product audit. Each one has great value to the client, the auditor, and the auditee. There is interaction between the three types of audits. These audits will be discussed in chapter 2.

To save time and avoid embarrassment, before performing an audit, auditors must know the quality standards/specifications against which they are auditing. Usually, there are at least two types of quality specifications. One type is overall general system requirements, for example, MIL-Q-9858A and ANSI/ISO/ASQC Q9000 standards. The second type is process or product quality specification criteria, for example, American Society for Testing and Materials (ASTM). Manuals and documents that delineate a company's quality program need to be reviewed in an audit. These include policy manuals, procedures, and work instructions.

Chapters 7, 8, and 9 define quality element criteria. These elements are a composite of general quality specifications. Managers can use the quality elements highlighted in these chapters as a guideline for implementation in an overall quality system. Auditors could use these elements to develop audit checklists and to verify what was agreed upon by sales or contractual agreements.

If audits are carried out with the proper planning, on-site performance evaluation, reporting, and closure phases, they can be used to enhance quality systems. Audits provide a mechanism for establishing trusting relationships within a company, as well as with internal and external suppliers, customers, and clients.

Chapter 2

Audit Definitions and Applications

In order to clarify the terms used in quality auditing and their application, this chapter defines the terminology and techniques used by quality auditors.

Quality Audit Definition

"A systematic and independent examination to determine whether quality activities and related results comply with planned arrangements and whether these arrangements are implemented effectively and are suitable to achieve objectives."[1]

Types of Audits

System Audit

"A documented activity performed to verify, by examination and evaluations of objective evidence, that applicable elements of the quality system are appropriate and have been developed, documented, and effectively implemented in accordance and in conjunction with specified requirements."[2]

A quality system audit is a review of the quality management system. It looks at the functional quality system elements (see chapters 7, 8, and 9) and assesses whether or not a company has a quality management system in place and the ability to comply with contractual agreements and preestablished internal policy statements. By looking at the documented quality assurance program, the auditor assesses the documentation, implementation, and effectiveness of these quality system elements and verifies that a quality system exists and is being followed.

Process Audit

A process audit evaluates established procedures. It is an audit of in-process controls of operations or a series of operations. It verifies that process procedures and work instructions exist, that they are appropriate, and that they are being followed under standard conditions, rushed conditions, and adverse conditions.

Product Audit

A product audit is the reinspection of a product that has gone through final inspection. The product audit is an assessment of the inspection process, which includes the correct use of the specifications and the capability of the inspector to use proper judgment in determining the acceptability of the product. In addition, it is the reverification that product characteristics are being met.

There is some confusion when products are measured for acceptability to product specifications during an audit as to whether it should be considered a product audit or process audit. In general, in-line sample auditing of product characteristics is considered a process audit, as the analysis of the product during production illustrates the process performance. If the product is in a completed stage of production and has passed final inspection, it is considered a product audit.

Compliance Audit

A compliance audit is performed after a quality system audit has established that a quality system exists. It investigates whether or not the quality management system is still in place, is being implemented, and is effective. It dissects particular parts of a quality system audit and measures the effectiveness of a quality system to comply with contractual and specification requirements. A compliance audit looks at compliance to standards, reviews the processes, and reviews the data of those processes. "Only the compliance audit can assess the real efficacy of the quality management system and determine where improvement is possible or corrective action is needed."[3]

Survey

A survey is a comprehensive evaluation that analyzes such things as facilities, resources, economic stability, technical capability, personnel, production capabilities, and past performance, as well as the entire quality system. In general, a survey is performed prior to the award of a contract to a prospective supplier to ensure that the proper capabilities and quality system are in place. A product audit could be part of a process audit and a process audit could be part of a system audit. Due to the fact that a survey evaluates additional items not necessarily included in a quality system audit, such as economic stability, a survey is more encompassing than a quality system audit (see Figure 2.1).

Internal Audit

This is also referred to as a *first-party audit.* It is performed by a company on itself, using one of its own staff or a specialist contractor as auditor.[4]

External Audit—Second Party

An external audit, also called a *second-party audit*, is performed on a supplier or potential supplier by the customer or by another party or organization on behalf of the customer.[5]

External Audit—Third Party

A company may hire an individual or an organization to perform an audit with the objective of obtaining independent registration in compliance with a particular standard. Mandatory audits initiated by government regulatory agencies, such as the Environmental Protection Agency (EPA) or the State Department of Health and Welfare are also third-party audits.

Management Review

A management review is an internal review by management to ensure that a system of processes, procedures, and controls that affect quality exists and is appropriate, up-to-date, and adequate in relation to quality policy and objectives.

Operational Audit

An operational audit ensures that unit activities reach the economic and performance goals established by managers. An operational audit utilizes such methods as time studies and work studies to establish

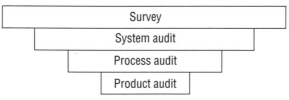

Figure 2.1. Hierarchy of audits.

that employees are performing their jobs in accordance with preestablished time and procedural requirements.[6]

Readiness Review

A readiness review is an internal management review of a company's compliance to standards and regulations prior to a second-party, third-party, or mandated state or federal audit. It allows the company to evaluate its status and compliance to operational requirements and standards. An example of this is a review by a company's management of its compliance to safety standards prior to an Occupational Safety and Health Administration (OSHA) evaluation.

Characteristics of an Audit

Independent of Doer

An audit must be performed by someone not directly responsible for production in the area being audited. Audit information needs to be objective and impartial. "Quality audits are carried out by staff not having direct responsibility in the areas being audited but, preferably, working in cooperation with the relevant personnel."[7]

Second- and third-party external audits should always follow the rule of independent of doer, however, in this author's opinion, during a first-party audit, employees versed in the use of quality auditing can perform periodic mini-self-assessments within their own unit to ensure compliance to contracts, standards, regulations, policies, processes, and work instruction requirements. Who can better bring to light nonconformances or inadequacies of the system than the people versed in auditing principles and techniques who are involved with the planning, implementing, performing, and monitoring of the process on a daily basis?

Measurement Criteria

Measurement criteria establish the standards the auditor is auditing against and to what extent compliance is exhibited. This is done through the use of data collection during an audit. There are two primary methods of data collection—attributes and variables—and auditors should recognize the difference between them. Attributes data collection uses a system of acceptable/nonacceptable or go/no-go. Variables data collection uses actual measurements of the items being evaluated. Variables data give more precise information and may be used for a trend analysis of processes. It may require more time and the use of more meticulous measurements.

Competent Personnel

Audit personnel must be trained and qualified in the art and science of quality auditing. Qualification requires a combination of training and experience. Training programs should be established, documented, and reviewed periodically.

Cost-Effectiveness

The audit program should be cost-effective and should emphasize the prevention of problems before they occur to reduce unnecessary costs. It is often helpful to incorporate the quality auditing functions into a quality cost system. The components of a quality cost system are

- *Prevention costs*—The costs of all activities specifically designed to prevent poor quality in products or services. The cost of second- and third-party audits would be categorized as a prevention cost.
- *Appraisal costs*—The costs associated with evaluating or auditing products or services to ensure conformance to quality standards and performance requirements. First-party internal audits could be categorized as either a prevention or appraisal cost, depending upon their usage and intent.
- *Internal failure costs*—Failure costs occurring prior to shipment or delivery of the product or service to the customer.
- *External failure costs*—Failure costs occurring after delivery or shipment of the product or the service to the customer, which are typically discovered by the customer.

A separate account should be established to monitor the costs of the audit program and the successful effect it has on a company. Further definitions of quality costs classifications can be found in Appendix B.

Sampling Process

A sample of the system is like a snapshot in time, which isolates one particular moment. It is similar to shining a spotlight on a forest of trees and drawing a conclusion about all of the trees based on the appearance of the highlighted trees. We must be very sure the sampling procedure is correct in order to avoid making incorrect assumptions.

There are four assumptions that can be deduced from sampling.

- Something is assumed to be acceptable when it is actually acceptable.
- Something is assumed to be unacceptable when it is actually unacceptable.
- Something is assumed to be unacceptable when it is actually acceptable. This is a Type I error (alpha error). In this type of error we would actually reject acceptable items.
- Something is assumed to be acceptable when it is actually unacceptable. This is a Type II error (beta error). In this type of error, we would accept items that are below our quality standards.

In order to avoid Type I and Type II errors, a lot of thought must go into sample planning. Proper consideration must be given to sample size, sample amount, location of sample(s), and sampling errors.

In many inspection sampling plans, most, if not all, of the following parameters are known: process capabilities, nonconformance rate, acceptable quality levels (AQLs), universe size, and lot size. Therefore, sampling standards such as the MIL-STD-105E, which are based on a continuous series of lots, may be used. Typically, however, an auditor does not have the luxury of knowing the parameters of the area being audited, so the use of sampling standards such as MIL-STD-105E should be avoided.

Use of Audits

Audits should be used for the continuous quality improvement effort, both externally and internally. They should not be used for acceptance of a product where capabilities of a process may not be known; nor should they be used to make a bad example of a company. All discoveries on an audit should remain confidential among the client, the auditor, and the auditee.

A code of ethics has been established by ASQC and is contained in the ASQC certification booklet. It reads as follows:

Code of Ethics

To uphold and advance the honor and dignity of the profession, and in keeping with high standards of ethical conduct, I acknowledge that I:

Fundamental Principles

I. *Will be honest and impartial; will serve with devotion my employer, my clients, and the public.*

II. *Will strive to increase the competence and prestige of the profession.*

III. *Will use my knowledge and skill for the advancement of human welfare and in promoting the safety and reliability of products for public use.*

IV. *Will earnestly endeavor to aid the work of the Society.*

Relations with the Public

1.1 *Will do whatever I can to promote the reliability and safety of all products that come within my jurisdiction.*

1.2 *Will endeavor to extend public knowledge of the work of the Society and its members that relates to the public welfare.*

1.3 *Will be dignified and modest in explaining my work and merit.*

1.4 *Will preface any public statements that I may issue by clearly indicating on whose behalf they are made.*

Relations with Employers and Clients

2.1 *Will act in professional matters as a faithful agent or trustee for each employer or client.*

2.2 *Will inform each client or employer of any business connections, interests, or affiliations that might influence my judgment or impair the equitable character of my services.*

2.3 *Will indicate to my employer or client the adverse consequences to be expected if my professional judgment is overruled.*

2.4 *Will not disclose information concerning the business affairs or technical processes of any present or former employer or client without his or her consent.*

2.5 *Will not accept compensation from more than one party for the same service without the consent of all parties. If employed, I will engage in supplementary employment of consulting practice only with the consent of my employer.*

Relations with Peers

3.1 *Will take care that credit for the work of others is given to those to whom it is due.*

3.2 *Will endeavor to aid the professional development and advancement of those in my employ or under my supervision.*

3.3 *Will not compete unfairly with others; will extend my friendship and confidence to all associates and those with whom I have business relations.*[8]

The goals and intent of the audit program can greatly affect how audits are performed. The following are some reasons for the establishment of an audit program.

- *Competition*—The ability to perform management audits provides a company with a mechanism to monitor, both internally and externally, its quality system. This gives a company a competitive edge in the business market.

  Through the external audit, we look for low-cost, high-value suppliers. Ideally, we want suppliers who will add value to our products (utility). Through the internal audit, we seek to verify that our quality system is adequate and effective. Ideally, the quality system should be striving for reduced variation of products and/or services by identifying the most effective way of performing the process, documenting the process and procedures, and ensuring that they are being followed. The internal audit verifies that this is or is not taking place.

- *Regulations*—Regulations may require a company to establish an internal and/or external quality audit program.

- *Self-Imposed Audits*—Self-imposed audits are established by company policy or internal regulations. Remember, auditing may be used as a tool for self-preservation. Audit one's self before someone else does. A good practice is to perform a preaudit assessment of a facility to ascertain if safety requirements are being met before OSHA comes in to evaluate them. If OSHA discovers nonconformances, fines may be assessed.

Audits can be valuable tools for evaluating a company's performance if they

- Meet management needs by providing feedback on areas in need of improvement.

- Provide a look forward in time by predicting where process controls or product measurements are needed.

- Measure effectiveness and compliance to internal and external policy and contract requirements.

Knowing our customers' needs is essential for an effective quality audit as the audit is our product or service, which is expressed by the final audit report. In order to satisfy the needs of our customers, we need to know who our customers are. In the case of an external audit, the customer is the client: the buyer of the audit service. In the case of an internal audit, the customer is the boss or manager who gives the authority to perform the audit. In either instance, the auditee is considered the customer as well. If we keep in mind who our customers are on an audit, our audit effectiveness will be increased.

What Do Managers Do?

Managers are responsible for the entire system and its various processes. This responsibility includes the design of the product or service, the measurement of the amount of trouble with the product or service, and the assignment of responsibility for action to remove the cause of the problem.[9]

The Deming cycle (named after W. Edwards Deming) is a method that can aid management in the pursuit of continuous and neverending process improvement.[10] The Deming cycle was originally known as the Shewhart cycle after its founder, Walter A. Shewhart, in 1950. It contains four segments: plan-do-check-act (PDCA).[11]

In recent years, the cycle has been refined to read plan-do-study-act or plan-do-monitor-act. Within this cycle, auditing provides a mechanism for monitoring the system. It is difficult to manage something if it is not monitored. Auditing provides one method of monitoring so that corrective actions may be implemented.

In general, there are four phases of an audit. The following is a guideline for the time frame for each of the phases.

Phase 1—Initiation and preparation—a minimum of 25 percent of the total time allocated for the audit

Phase 2—Performance phase—approximately 50 percent of the total time allocated for the audit

Phases 3 and 4—Audit reporting and closure—approximately 25 percent of the total time allocated for the audit

The next three chapters will describe each of the four phases of an audit.

Endnotes

1. ANSI/ISO/ASQC Q10011-1-1994, 5.

2. ANSI/ASQC QI-1986, 2.

3. Sayle, *Management Audits*, 5.

4. Quality Management International, *Quality System Auditor Training Course Manual*.

5. Ibid.

6. Sawyer, *The Practice of Modern Internal Auditing*, 4.

7. ANSI/ISO/ASQC Q10011-1-1994, 1.

8. ASQC, *Auditor Certification*, 9.

9. Gitlow, et al., *Tools and Methods*, 18, 19.

10. Ibid.

11. Deming, *Out of the Crisis*, 88–89.

Chapter 3

Phase 1—Audit Initiation and Preparation

Audit Initiation

Audits are initiated by the client, who determines the need for, the purpose of, the type of, and the objectives of the audit. Typically, the lead auditor arranges what will be included in the audit plan, and the client makes the final decision on the plan's contents.[1] The time allocated for an audit is critical, therefore, proper planning is important.

Consider these actions: identify the scope of audit to be performed, gather information, select audit team members, and determine the standards or documents with which the auditee's quality system is required to comply. A preliminary evaluation, or desk audit, of the auditee's quality system should be performed and should include a review of such documents as the quality assurance policy manual. A desk audit of the quality assurance system is described later in this chapter.

Audit Preparation

Audit Objectives

It is imperative in the planning stage of an audit that the audit team be well-versed in the types of quality and product specifications the auditee is using to establish compliance. It is important for the auditor to determine which quality requirements have been imposed on the auditee before the audit is performed. Objectives should be stated regarding the purpose of the audit, which may include initial evaluation of a potential supplier or verification of a quality system to meet specific requirements. Quality assurance systems and product standards, such as company manuals, department procedures, and process instructions, need to be identified and included in the audit objectives.

Scope

The scope of the audit should determine what facilities, products, processes, system elements, departments, or activities will be covered. To develop the scope of the audit, a preliminary visit to the auditee may be needed. Clearly defined boundaries should be established at this point. Some considerations are

- Determine which product lines are to be included in the scope of the audit.
- Determine what elements of the quality standards are to be included in the scope of the audit. An example of an element that might be included would be the procurement element. The auditor would need to verify that the auditee has a system in place that monitors the subsuppliers' quality system. This evaluation would be included in the scope of the audit.
- Determine where the processes and products being audited are geographically located. This can avoid the potentially embarrassing situation of being on location and discovering that additional processes that need to be audited are in other geographic locations, thereby precluding the auditor from completing the audit.

Resources

The group responsible for performing the audit should have a documented, formalized program that includes the selection, training, and monitoring (such as periodic review of qualifications) of all auditors. The actual audit team participants should be assigned according to their qualifications and expertise. Audit team members with diverse areas of expertise can break up into miniteams on a large audit to analyze different elements of the quality system simultaneously. If members of the quality audit team are in the training or educational stage, they may slow the audit. Additionally, technical specialists may often be asked to accompany the audit team to lend their knowledge of the specific product or service line being audited. The lead auditor must ensure that the audit proceeds according to the planned time frame, as the technical specialist may not be versed in the audit process.

Lead Auditor. The audit team is supervised by the lead auditor, who is ultimately responsible for all phases of the audit. The lead auditor's responsibilities include preparing the audit plan, briefing the audit team and the auditee, submitting the audit report, and, in most cases, selecting other audit team members and their assignments.

Auditor. The auditor is a part of the audit team that supports the lead auditor during the evaluation. A good auditor possesses the following characteristics.[2]

- Knowledge of quality, production, engineering, and procurement principles and practices
- Knowledge of requirements
- Knowledge of techniques (such as interviewing and statistical techniques)
- Sound judgment/open-mindedness
- Patience
- Interest
- Tenacity (strength)
- Professional attitude/integrity
- Good listening skills
- Inquisitiveness
- Good verbal and written skills
- Analytical skills
- Honesty
- Ethics
- Diplomacy
- Discipline
- Good planning skills
- Experience
- Objectivity
- Empathy

Undesirable characteristics include being[3]

- Argumentative
- Opinionated
- Lazy
- Easily influenced
- Inflexible

- Impulsive—jumps to conclusions
- Gullible
- Uncommunicative
- Devious
- Poor at planning
- Unprofessional
- Prescriptive

Team Size

To ensure corroboration of statements, documents, and data viewed and/or collected during the audit, audit teams should have more than one auditor. This adds to the total knowledge of the audit team and provides verification and support of items evaluated during an audit. In some cases, the use of one auditor may be acceptable, particularly on an internal product or process audit; however, this may present a problem when verification of undocumented items or corroboration from other team members is needed.

It is important to have a well-balanced audit team, but too large a team may become unwieldy. Usually the auditee provides audit team members with escorts to the various areas being audited. Even when auditors combine to form miniteams, too many people in one location make answering evaluation questions difficult and intimidating for the auditee. To avoid chaos, no more than six members should comprise an audit team and no more than two auditors should interview an individual at any given time. If the audit team is large enough, they should split up into miniteams to make the audit more efficient.

Time Elements Involved in an Audit

Try to stick to the plan. An audit contains a width and a depth. In general, the length of time required to perform an audit will depend upon the number of audit team members, the size of the facility, the number of verifications required, and the scope (width) and thoroughness (depth) of the audit. A typical system audit performed at a facility requires between one to five days. The following guidelines are recommended.

- If the auditee has fewer than 500 employees, the audit should take one to three days.
- If the auditee has 500–1000 employees, the audit should take four to five days.

Note: Employee population is defined as the number of employees working in the area to be covered by the scope of the audit, and may not necessarily include the total number of employees working at the facility. Adjust the number of audit team members according to the scope, thoroughness, and size of the facilities in an effort to stay within the suggested time required for the audit.

Process or product audits may require less time to perform as they are typically more thorough in their depth (concentrating on particular areas), but are limited in regards to the width (the scope).

Initial Contact

After being given the authority to perform the audit by the client, the lead auditor should make the initial contact. A telephone call, followed by a letter, should be made stating the purpose and scope of the audit, the confirmation of the date and time of arrival, the names and titles of the audit team members, and an indication as to what quality production specifications, quality system specifications, or contractual requirements the audit scope will cover. The letter should also include a request that organizational charts and/or quality policy manuals be sent to the audit team prior to the visit.[4]

Understand the Systems of the Areas You Are Auditing

What Are the Controls of the System?

Prior to the on-site audit, a desk audit of the quality assurance system is performed to determine what control system is in place. One way this can be done is by looking at the quality assurance policy manual. One easy way to perform a desk audit of a quality assurance policy manual is to write in the margin areas of concern that will be investigated during the on-site evaluation. The following abbreviations can be used.

V—Items that need verification.

?—Items that need clarification.

W—"Weasel Words"—Descriptive words or phrases that are vague where more precise parameters are to be indicated. (For example, properly, snugly, thin or thick, securely).

In addition, the auditor might look at the organizational charts and process and procedure manuals to investigate the history of the performance of the products and/or services. The investigation should include an evaluation of prior audits and verification that the previous corrective actions have remained in effect and that previously recorded strengths are still in place. Any changes or exemptions (waivers) requested in the past should be reviewed. Records of past problems, isolated incidences, or common occurrences should be evaluated.

The auditor looks at what facts are available, who generates them, the frequency of the generation, who reviews the facts, how corrective actions are initiated based on the facts, how key variables are identified, and what is used to monitor processes (such as statistics or capability studies). The auditor then develops an audit checklist based on the information obtained during the desk audit and the understanding of the control systems in the areas being audited.

Audit Checklists

The checklist provides working papers upon which the data collected by the audit team are documented. It contains a list of specific questions pertaining to areas being evaluated during the audit. Checklists provide structure and continuity to the audit and ensure that the scope of the audit is being followed.[5] It is helpful to have the audit team brainstorm ideas to develop and define the checklist before the audit. Checklists should not stifle creativity.

Checklists provide a means of communication, a place to record data to use for future reference, and help to manage the time and pace of an audit.[6] They also provide guidelines for the entire audit team so that quality elements being investigated are seen in a like manner by each team member. They should be standard enough to provide direction, but flexible enough to include additional areas as questions arise.

Developing Checklist Questions

Checklist questions should be developed that drive the auditor to determine the answers to the following questions.

- What is the process during standard operations?
- What is the process during nonstandard or rushed conditions?
- What is the process when there is a problem or emergency situation, and how are these difficulties handled?

Typically, in their operating procedures, most companies take into account times when everything is running as it normally should under normal conditions.

The auditor's questions should reflect that variations in standard practices may occur during certain time frames, such as at the end of the month or during different shifts. The audit checklist should generate questions that verify that these circumstances are covered by an auditee's internal procedures when nonstandard or rushed conditions occur. In addition, during panic-stricken times, some companies throw their standard operating procedures out the window and do not have internal controls and procedures that are followed to handle these crisis circumstances.

For example, in the health care field, when auditing a long-term care facility, the audit checklist should include questions that drive the auditor to investigate practices for patient care on various shifts during standard conditions of operation. A nonstandard condition might be when there are a lot of call-offs from regular nursing staff and agency nurses who are not familiar with the patients are sent to the facility. The checklist should contain questions that allow the auditor to investigate how the facility provides consistent patient care through standardized procedures during such conditions. Another example would be an emergency situation with a patient where nursing staff would be required to follow emergency procedures that supersede their standard operating practices.

Types of Checklist Questions

The lead auditor decides which type of checklist questions would be the most beneficial for use on the audit.

- Canned or standard checklists contain preexisting questions on particular topics.[7] There are numerous auditing books on the market that provide standard checklists, such as the *Quality Assurance Evaluator's Workbook* by L. Marvin Johnson.
- Checklists that ask open-ended questions give the auditor the flexibility of documenting objective evidence verified during the audit.[8]
- Attribute checklists are those that contain questions that are answered in a yes/no, go/no-go, or compliance/noncompliance fashion.[9] This type of checklist efficiently documents data collected during an audit in a manner that is easy to read. One drawback to this type of checklist occurs when an audit of an area reveals partial compliance and a yes/no answer may not give the full picture.
- Variable checklists allow for graded or numerical ratings. This type of checklist gives the auditor flexibility to document the gray areas when partial compliance is achieved

and to establish a hierarchy of compliance through the use of ratings.

In summary, during the preparation phase, the audit objectives are defined, the audit scope is established, resources are allocated, the auditee is contacted, checklists are developed, the auditee's history is reviewed, and an understanding of the auditee's process and control systems has taken place. A properly executed preparation phase should provide the auditor with the following results: an audit plan, audit checklists, an initial evaluation based on the desk audit, historical data and past performance, and a plan of action for areas needing verification during the on-site phase of the audit.[10]

Endnotes

1. ANSI/ISO/ASQC Q10011-1, 1994, 4.

2. Johnson, *Quality Assurance Program Evaluation*, 43–47.

3. Ibid.

4. Sayle, *Management Audits*, 9.

5. ASQC Energy Division, *Nuclear Auditor Training Handbook*, 42.

6. Arter, *Quality Audits for Improved Performance*, 7.

7. Ibid., 31–34.

8. Ibid.

9. Ibid.

10. Ibid., 36.

Chapter 4

Phase 2—Performance of an Audit: On-Site Evaluation

One of the most important aspects of an audit is the actual on-site evaluation of an organization's quality program. Audits can be stressful for both the auditor and the auditee. Uncertainty of areas to be covered and a limited amount of time add to the stress. A preparation phase that is properly planned and communicated ultimately lessens the stress created by the audit and provides a smoother transition to the on-site performance.

Opening Meeting

At the beginning of the performance phase, an opening meeting should be held. Those in attendance should include the entire audit team, the auditee's plant manager, and the organization's appropriate staff members, including the quality assurance manager.

It is important that two-way communication be established at the opening meeting. Introductions are made, and objectives are restated concerning the audit scope and the quality and product specifications to which the company is being audited. Logistics of the audit are planned at this time, including the auditee's hours of operation, escorts to be used during the audit, tentative schedules, and room availability for team meetings, daily briefings, and the exit meeting. In addition, audit checklists are distributed. This meeting need not be longer than 30 minutes.

Two important factors for the audit team to remember are to be on time and to dress appropriately for this meeting. Dressing appropriately means making a professional first impression. During subsequent days of the audit, however, the auditors will need to dress according to the environment. A good rule of thumb is that auditors should dress one notch above the employees in the area being audited.

If requested by the client, the opening meeting should allow sufficient time for a review of previous audit observations and corrective actions that needed to be taken. If the company would like to have a forum to discuss enhancements within their continuous quality improvement systems, set some time aside for this as well.

On-Site Evaluation

Auditors can be compared to florists. A florist collects flowers, puts them into a basket, makes a flower arrangement, and delivers the arrangement.[1] The auditor collects the evidence, puts it on the worksheets, arranges the data, and delivers the report.

After auditing for more than six hours per day an auditor tends to lose efficiency, although most audits take at least eight hours per day to perform. Keeping this in mind, schedule an audit of the more difficult areas during the first six hours of the audit process. For example, start the day by evaluating the manufacturing processes and end the day reviewing the purchasing function.

Primary Causes of Quality Issues

There are several primary causes of quality issues.[2] They are

- Lack of top management support
- Lack of organization
- Lack of training
- Lack of discipline
- Lack of resources
- Lack of time
- Lack of teamwork
- Lack of knowledge
- Lack of consistency

The auditor is looking for symptoms of these issues.

Collection, Evaluation, and Verification of Control Systems

When evaluating the quality system, an auditor needs to keep in mind that there are formal and informal control systems. An auditor should not feel that everything should be documented in a formal system just to make the auditor's job simple. Some wonderful control systems can exist that are not documented. It is the auditor's responsibility to find out how these informal systems are being used and if they need to be documented.

The auditor needs to establish, through verification, the answers to these questions.

1. Does top management believe in quality?
2. Are quality goals transmitted throughout the company?
3. Is the control system used by management adequate and effective?
4. Are key variables that impact quality identified?
5. Is the control system working?
6. How is it monitored?

If the system is in place, quality will follow. To verify the system is in place, three primary methods are used: tracing, corroboration, and sampling. This chapter will discuss tracing and corroboration. Chapter 11 will discuss sampling.

Audit Paths (Tracing)

There are four primary paths an auditor may follow in seeking factual evidence. Each has advantages and disadvantages. One of the skills of the auditor is to select the most appropriate path for each audit situation. Each path will be considered in turn.[3]

Tracing a Contract. This method is often used by second-party auditors carrying out a series of audits on a contract as the contract progresses. Second-party auditors are primarily concerned with the control being exercised on their particular job. Their interest in the quality system is confined to the impact on the contract. This method of auditing provides a high level of assurance to the customer that the contract is proceeding satisfactorily. The auditor must be knowledgeable about the contract conditions. This method is ideal when an order is in place, but the information obtained is essentially of use only to the customer.

Random Auditing. The advantages of this method of auditing are that there is always plenty to see and the auditee will have little chance of knowing what the auditor intends to look at. This type of audit tends to investigate what is actually taking place at the time of the audit; therefore, work reflects current procedures. The disadvantage is that there is no pattern to the audit, and the auditor can become disorientated through continually having to deal with new contracts and situations. This method is often used by third-party auditors for certification audits and surveillance.

Tracing the Flow of Work (Horizontal Auditing). This combines some of the advantages of the previous two methods. Backward tracing of the work allows the auditor to examine work that is currently taking place or recently completed. Through examining historic records, process controls, process inputs, training instructions, and records, work can be traced back to the earlier processes and source material. Tracing the flow of work allows the interfaces between processes and departments to be examined in detail.

Forward tracing of work has the same advantages as backward tracing with the additional plus that the auditor follows the flow of work in its natural sequence. The disadvantage is that it is not until the end of the investigation that the auditor actually sees the output of all the processes that are being investigated.

Tracing work is a technique used by internal, second-, and third-party auditors.

Vertical Auditing. Policy and directives emanating from the chief executive officer (CEO) and senior management have to be interpreted and implemented by successive layers of managers, supervisors, and operators throughout the organization. Vertical auditing, starting at the highest level, is an effective way to measure how well this is done. Quality policy is a case in point. The auditor can see how well the policy has been communicated, implemented, and understood in each department and whether objectives and targets are being met. This method can be used to particular effect during internal audits. It is also a useful technique in second- and third-party audits.

In addition to the four previously mentioned audit paths, the following tracing methods may also be used. *Departmental tracing* reviews numerous quality elements within a department. In *element tracing*, the auditor reviews a quality element in various departments.

To a large extent the auditor will have decided the audit path to be adopted for each phase of the audit. Some functions/departments lend themselves naturally to one particular approach. For example, vertical auditing is used to examine quality policy and its implementation; calibration is always conducted by random audit; and tracking techniques lend themselves to situations where there is a natural flow of work such as design offices and production areas. The advantages and disadvantages and use of these audit paths are summarized in Table 4.1.

Path	Use	Advantages	Disadvantages
Tracking a contract	Primarily second party	Effective method to provide information on a contract. High level of assurance obtained.	Results are useful only to the customer.
Backward tracking (horizontal)	Third-party, second-party, and internal audits	Can start anywhere in the flow of work. Output of the process can be seen before the process and inputs are examined. Examines interfaces.	Audit slows if people or information are not readily available. Inflexible. Not logical.
Forward tracking (horizontal)	Third-party, second-party, and internal audits	Follows the flow of work. Can start anywhere. Logical. Examines interfaces.	Audit slows if people or information are not available. Inflexible.
Random	Primarily used by third-party auditors for certification audits and surveillance	Lots of work to examine. Auditee cannot anticipate what the auditor will be examining. Examines current work and procedures.	There is no pattern to the audit. Auditor is faced with new situations and audit is disjointed.
Vertical	Primarily internal audits but also limited use by third-party and second-party audits to measure commitment.	Effectively measures implementation of policy, directives, and objectives.	Requires experienced auditors. Difficult to do.

Quality Management International, Inc., Exton, PA 1994. Used with permission.

Table 4.1. Audit Paths.

Corroboration

Since it is a fact that perceptions vary from individual to individual, corroboration ensures that facts stated or data collected during an audit are accurate. It is always better to have statements made during an interview corroborated by someone else who has been asked the same questions and/or verified by documentation. The facts must agree based upon at least two different auditors, two different records, two different interviews, or any combination of these.

Tangible conclusions are recorded in the form of qualitative or quantitative reporting. *Qualitative reporting* is a general overview of a performance level. *Quantitative reporting* is a precise measurement of the total number of articles investigated versus the total number of noncompliances. An example would be the investigation of purchasing order agreements. A report stating that some purchase orders do not have the product specifications on them would be a qualitative verification statement. A report stating that, out of 50 purchasing order documents, five did not contain the full product specifications would be a quantitative statement.

Data Collection

There are four primary sources of data collection.

- *Physical evidence.* Physical evidence is represented by tangible data that are verified during the audit. Examples are the testing, retesting, and evaluations done by the auditee organization to their product or service to ensure verification of conformance.

- *Sensory observation.* Sensory observation includes verification of the system through the use of your five senses. Visual clues would include parts or tags on the floor, rusty nails on the floor, or the observation of tasks being performed. An example of an auditory clue would be the out-of-the-ordinary clanging of a machine, which may lead to the questioning of the facility's maintenance and the machine's ability to produce a satisfactory product.

- *Comparisons and trends.* Auditors look for patterns and trends of occurrences that may stem from systematic or isolated causes. An example of a pattern would be where 50 percent of drawings or constructions are consistently released in several areas of the operation without proper approval.

- *Interviews and questioning.* Interviews and questioning conducted at all levels of the company's staffing is one of the most important sources of data collection. Questions should be asked in a way that does not imply sexism or bias. The following five-step method is recommended for an effective interview.[4]

  1. Put the person at ease by making the person being interviewed part of the audit process. One way to accomplish this is to concentrate on the audit checklist by asking for input in response to the checklist. The interview itself should be conducted in a relatively quiet area, which may need to be away from the immediate worksite. In certain instances where the actual procedures and processes must be demonstrated, however, the interview may need to be held on the worksite.

  2. Explain the purpose of your presence. Demonstrate knowledge, competence, and caring through the types of questions you ask and through your knowledge of the facility and product or services, but avoid being perceived as a know-it-all.

  3. Use proper questioning techniques. As an auditor, realize that people sometimes do not hear a question properly and/or may not manage to say what they really want to say. One type of question that is most effective is an open-ended one. An example of this type is "What did you have for breakfast?" as opposed to "Did you have coffee, eggs, and toast?"

     Another effective technique is asking "Why" five consecutive times until you reach the fundamental answer to the question. In addition, the five Ws and a *how* may be used— what, where, when, why, who, and how, if appropriate.

     Make sure you use your two ears and one mouth. Listen twice as much as you talk.

     If, after trying these techniques, you are still not receiving proper feedback, you might try a technique known as the pregnant pause. In this technique you try to break the existing barrier between you and the person being questioned by stepping closer into that individual's space, staring into his or her eyes, asking the question, and then waiting patiently for the response.

4. Verify what is said. Look for data and ask for data. Believe a confession and verify a claim. State your conclusions by writing your notes out loud. Do not keep your thoughts a secret or withhold information. Be flexible and allow room for additional information and discussion. Clarify what you are told. Repeat the response. Try not to argue. Remember, if you are arguing with a fool, someone walking by would not know which one the fool is.

5. Conduct a cordial conclusion to the interview and explain any necessary follow-up.

Briefing the Auditee

While the audit is in process, approximately five to 10 minutes should be set aside with the auditee in each area to review issues particular to that area. Verifications that were made and any concerns by the audit team should be discussed at this time to give the auditee a second chance to provide any factual data that may have been omitted.

Team Meetings

At the end of each audit day, the team leader should hold a meeting with all the audit team members to review the day's work. The facts/verifications, observations, tentative conclusions, and issues encountered are discussed with the entire audit team. Based upon this review, a replanning of the audit schedule may be necessary. A brief summary report of the day is then compiled at the conclusion of the team meeting. The audit team leader should decide whether there is a need to review the status of the audit with the auditee.

Endnotes

1. Arter, *Quality Audits for Improved Performance*, 28.

2. Sayle, *Management Audits*, 1–5.

3. Quality Management International, *Quality System Auditor Training Course*, 4–7.

4. Arter, *Quality Audits for Improved Performance*, 43–47.

Chapter 5

Phases 3 and 4—Reporting and Closure Phases

There are two types of reporting: the formal and the informal. Both types of reporting need to be clear and precise.

Reporting

The exit meeting occurs at the completion of the on-site audit and is an example of the informal type of reporting. It is usually a verbal account of the results of the audit to the auditee's management and the auditee's appropriate personnel and may be accompanied by a rough written report. Approximately one hour should be set aside for this exit meeting.

A formal report follows with a written document to the auditee and should be submitted no later than two weeks from the time the audit is completed. Although it may be desirable to submit the report within two weeks for external audits, it may not be practical due to the time necessary to secure approvals through the proper channels.

In general, observations during the on-site phase (that is, audit working papers, checklists, and so forth) may be either positive or negative. Once observations are recorded in the final formal audit report, however, the deficiencies take on a negative connotation, at which point the words *observation, finding,* and *nonconformance* become synonymous.

The writing of the *statement of nonconformance* is a critical part of the audit, as it challenges the auditee's system. Therefore, nonconformity statements must be written in a clear and factual manner.

One way to organize the nonconformity statement is as follows:

1. State the requirements of the internal or external standard.
2. State the department and/or geographic location where the nonconformity occurred.
3. State the factual evidence to support the nonconformance.
4. State the type of nonconformance with reference to the internal or external standard, procedure, or element with which it does not comply.

Exit Meeting

The exit meeting with the audit team and auditee must occur after the completion of the on-site audit. Attendance at this meeting is limited to the managers of the areas audited, upper management (which may include the president of the organization), and the quality manager. The quality manager alone may not be sufficient. If there are no major nonconformances to report, the auditee's upper management need not be present.

The lead auditor should present the summary and read the entire list of observations discovered on the audit without interruption from the auditees. Systems deficiencies and action items relating to the standards or requirements are stated. If a review of a particular observation needs to be revisited, the auditor responsible for the audit of that area and the lead auditor would then field questions pertaining to that particular observation. Observations should have been verified by this time, so that a strong position can be maintained in the case of a disagreement. If the verification of the observations of the audit team are not substantial enough to support the audit team's view in the disagreement, however, then a lesser degree of severity should be considered, or, in certain instances, the observations withdrawn. Discussion of audit details takes place during the exit meeting, during which individual auditors clarify statements or respond to specific questions of the areas they have audited.

Audit observations should be consolidated and categorized by their appropriate element of nonconformance. Observations are stated according to the degree of severity. A three-tier system of reporting deficiencies is recommended.[1]

Tier 1—Most critical—A systemic deficiency that adversely affects the quality of the product or service and is in conflict with contractual or procedural requirements.

Tier 2— A lesser degree of severity, such as an isolated observation that is in conflict with contractual or procedural requirements, but does not represent a systemic deficiency.

Tier 3— The least severe, such as concerns that may not be part of the required quality system, but should be considered for continuous quality improvement.

The last part of the exit meeting contains an explanation of required follow-up and corrective action response by the auditee. Minutes of the meeting should be kept.

If you start to lose control of the exit meeting due to a rebuttal from the auditee's management, lower your voice and continue your audit evaluation. Emphasize that these were the results based on objective evidence and that time does not allow for further discussion. Inform the auditee that any objections to the audit nonconformances (findings) should be stated in writing upon submission of the corrective action response. Resume the audit evaluation and bring the meeting to a close.

Content of the Formal Report

The formal report summarizes the results of the audit. Standards for the format and content of the report should be established and followed, as it enhances reading and understanding the content. The report should be prepared by the lead auditor with input from the audit team. It may be reviewed by the management of the organization in which the audit was conducted prior to issuance in order to avoid factual errors and misunderstandings. Review of the draft should not unduly delay the completion of the audit nor the two-week target date of the issuance of the final audit report.

The formal report should include a definitive assessment of compliance with established standards accompanied by significant observations (findings) relative to the audit objectives plus sufficient and relevant information on evidence with explanation and comments. Observations should be ranked by importance and arranged in logical order.[2] The report summarizes the results of the audit. Further details are documented in the working papers.

The following items are included in the formal audit report.

- Purpose, objective, and scope of the audit.
- Details of the audit plan, auditors, dates, and organization in which the audit was conducted.
- Standards and reference documents against which the audit was conducted.
- Audit observations, supporting evidence, and associated findings, comments, and recommendations.
- Noteworthy recommendations for quality improvements. (Note: Although this may be acceptable for first-party audits, it remains a point of contention of whether to do so becomes too prescriptive in second- and third-party quality auditors. A rule of thumb is, when in doubt, don't.
- Request for a plan of corrective action to be submitted that addresses significant observations, isolated observations, and any other areas of concern.
- Distribution of formal audit report.

An audit report must be dated and signed by the lead auditor/ auditor. Management of the auditing organization reviews and approves the report prior to submitting it to the client. Distribution of the report is left to the discretion of the client.

When writing the audit report, avoid emotional words and phrases, a bias and slanted viewpoint, and distracting graphics. More than six to eight items requiring corrective action in Tiers 1 and 2 may overwhelm management and may not achieve the desired results.

Content of the Corrective Action Plan

The auditee's management should submit its plan of corrective action within 30–45 days. This plan should be reviewed by the lead auditor and evaluated for contractual and procedural compliance. The corrective plan of action is also evaluated for its ability to correct the root cause of the identified issues within the quality system and not simply the specific incidents of nonconformance detected by the audit team.

Implementing the methods used to correct the nonconformances is strictly the responsibility of the auditee's management. Lead auditors/auditors should not place themselves in a position where their independence is compromised by being prescriptive in their evaluation of the auditee's corrective action responses.

Auditors should try to avoid a situation where corrective action responses lead to a paper chase. Additional on-site visits to follow up corrective action may be required, without additional documentation.

The plan can be accepted, rejected, or partially accepted by either the client or the lead auditor, depending upon the particular audit process. If the client deems it necessary, the client will then authorize the audit team to perform a reaudit of corrective actions taken.

A letter of closure assessing the auditee's corrective action plan may be submitted to the client and/or auditee as is applicable. Content of the letter of closure should include the total acceptance, partial acceptance, or rejection of the plan of corrective action and guidance as to the timetable for any future actions that are necessary. The timing as to when a letter of closure is sent and to whom it is distributed will depend upon the internal policies and procedures of the auditor's company and the client. If no corrective action is needed, a letter of closure may be sent as the final step of the audit process, formally closing the audit.

Note: Reaudit may be performed by auditors other than the original audit team.

Records Retention

Where contractually or internally required by the auditor's organization, the lead auditor, auditor, or audit organization is responsible for custody and retention of audit documents and records. Properly retained working papers, reports, and other documents of an audit facilitate future audit planning, review of audit work, preparation of reports on the work of audit departments/groups, and proof of compliance with audit standards. Complete reports, including supplemental documents, should be retained at least until the next formal audit is complete, in order to provide evidence that the findings of an earlier audit have been identified, corrected, and maintained.

Retention of audit documents should be standardized regarding form, procedure, and content. Required confidentiality must be maintained. Authorized personnel should be given reasonable access to retained audit documents in order to support future audits or other justified purposes.

Avoiding Pitfalls

The following list illustrates some problems that hinder the general audit process and should be avoided.[3]

- Inadequate planning and preparation for the audit
- Inadequate communication with auditee prior to the audit
- Lack of a clearly defined scope (areas and elements to be audited)
- Lack of understanding of the standards, contractual requirements, quality system requirements, and product specification criteria against which the audit is being performed
- Lack of properly trained auditors, including auditors with inadequate technical skills and interviewing skills
- Prescriptive when evaluating corrective action responses
- Failure to reevaluate implemented corrective actions

Endnotes

1. Bethlehem Steel Corporation, *Supplier Excellence Program*, 1–3.
2. Arter, *Quality Audits for Improved Performance*, 15, 18.
3. Ibid.

Chapter 6

Establishing the Framework for an Audit Program

This chapter presents a guideline for the development and administration of a quality auditing program. Although primarily geared toward the establishment of an internal quality program, these components can also be used to develop an external quality program.

The reasons a company establishes an audit program will determine the policy and charter of the program. The nature and scope will be based on whether the program is developed for compliance purposes, such as a defense against customer audits or regulatory requirements, or for the purpose of continuous quality improvement of both supplier performances and internal quality enhancements.

Determining the Type of Audit Program

Upper managers of a company give the authority to establish an audit program and determine which staff person will be the administrator of the audit program. In certain instances, the manager of the QA department may be selected as the administrator of both the internal and external audit functions. In other instances, the manager of purchasing may be assigned to direct the external audit functions. Either can lead to successful auditing programs, as long as the policies and charters of the program are established, documented, and implemented.

The administrator of the audit program needs to sell management on the value of an auditing program. Some good sells are enhancement of product or process performance, increased sales, and the ability to seek additional markets due to the success of compliance with external audits, such as the ISO 9000 series of standards.

Management of an audit program is affected by executive management policies, customer requirements, company size, and the type of product or service produced by the company. In setting up or expanding an audit program, the following factors should be considered.

- Audit policy or charter
- Audit procedures, manuals, and workbooks
- Auditor staffing and training
- Audit records and retention[1]

Definition of Policy

The underlying purpose of the policy is to ensure that all decisions support company objectives and management strategy in a consistent manner. To institute a successful audit program, support of upper management is absolutely essential. The charter of the audit program should reiterate management's commitment to the audit program by documenting the audit policy and establishing the ground rules to which audits are performed. An effective audit policy contains

- Plans and objectives of upper management
- Consistency of purpose
- Flexibility to accommodate unusual or unforeseen conditions
- Establishment of the audit function's independence
- Establishment of authority for the audit program[2]

Audit Procedures

In order to communicate the audit program to all relevant staff and operating personnel, audit procedures are written that describe the program's objectives and provide guidance to both the auditors and auditees. The following factors are considered in developing effective audit procedures.

- Implementation and support of organizational policy and objectives
- A logical flow or sequence of actions
- Clear definitions as to who is responsible for accomplishing specified tasks
- Definition of methods, tools, and documents to be used
- Alternative courses of action when more than one outcome is possible
- The use of simple language; avoiding the use of adjectives and adverbs

An auditor's workbook and manual may be derived from the procedures and ground rules established by the audit program. The auditor's workbook may include general statistical techniques and audit questions that can be applied during most audits.

General Principles for the Administration of an Audit

Certain ground rules should be applied for consistency in effective auditing.

- *Objectivity.* The true independence of an audit is reflected by the objectivity and usage of verification methods on the audit. Auditors need to have the ability to say what needs to be said without fear of repercussion.

  Sometimes auditors are given information by employees of the company that is true, but may be detrimental to the security of the employee's job. Such information should be held in confidence with documentation of facts and names recorded in the auditor's working papers if verification is needed at a later date. The formal report will then contain the facts, but the names of the contributors are omitted.

- *Attack the problems and not the people.* As an auditor, you must realize that you are not always right; you are human too! Avoid conflict when confronted with a difference of opinions. Remember to
  - Collect your thoughts.
  - Be courteous and polite.
  - Comply with audit objectives.
  - Use verification methods.
  - Be prepared.

  If you cannot verify what you believe is true, consider retracting your statements and move on.

An auditor's objectivity cannot be compromised by giving direction to line personnel, directly writing procedures on processes being audited, or directly resolving nonconformances or noncompliances in areas being audited. To maintain independence, an auditor cannot have direct responsibility for corrective action measures. In certain instances during an internal audit, however, an auditor may be called on to give input into the corrective action process. In this case, the next time that area is audited, another auditor should be considered to maintain objectivity of the audit.

The Vital Few vs. the Trivial Many

Due to the limited time in an audit, auditors should identify the "vital few" as opposed to the "trivial many." This principle is used in TQM systems worldwide and is known as the *Pareto principle*, a term coined and popularized by J. M. Juran.

Audit Interference

The audit process will sometimes interfere with the normal work flow of the auditee. Proper planning and questioning techniques can help avoid an undue amount of interruption in operations.[3]

Safety must also be taken into consideration when questioning operators of machinery. If at all possible, interviews should be performed in an off-site quiet area, away from the machines, to expedite the audit process. In other instances, where the processes and procedures need to be verified at the job site, the interviews need to be performed on-site.

Confidentiality

Confidentiality of audit results must be maintained by auditors and all those connected with the audit program. Information gathered from audits is not to be shared from company to company.

Audit Staffing and Training

An audit administrator will obtain more effective results if the audit staff has been selected for its knowledge, experience, and training. Selection of audit staff members should also be done in accordance with the characteristics and personality traits previously described in chapter 3.

A training program established for the audit staff includes:[4]

- Knowledge of audit policies and procedures
- Knowledge of auditing and quality standards
- Participation in auditor training courses
- The use of an auditor's manual, if required
- On-the-job training
- Documentation skills
- Oral and written presentation skills

It is the responsibility of the management of the auditor's company to establish an auditor training and qualification program. To this end, there are several guidelines available that provide direction in the establishment of quality auditor training requirements, such as the ANSI/ISO/ASQC Q10011-2-1994 or the *Nuclear Quality Systems Auditor Training Handbook, 2nd edition,* which provides a form for documenting auditor qualifications.

Audit Records and Retention Program

A records retention program must be established by the audit organization. It should include documentation and quality records pertinent to the audit function, as well as a retention timetable. Records are categorized as either permanent or nonpermanent, and it is the responsibility of the audit function to determine which records are which. Permanent records should be kept for at least one audit cycle to provide follow-up and direction for future audits. An example of a permanent record is the final audit report. An example of a nonpermanent record is the on-site nonessential notes written during the audit.

It is the client's responsibility to maintain records of audits performed, as the client is responsible for delegating future audit assignments. Future assignments may be given to a different audit team or agency. When setting up the audit program, remember to include audits of the audit function.

The preceding chapters have provided an understanding of the definitions, applications, and administration of the audit function, as well as an understanding of the actual implementation of the audit process. The next three chapters will explore the elements that comprise a total quality system. In addition, Appendix B expounds on the categories described in Element 21, quality costs, located in chapter 9.

In order to properly evaluate a company's total quality system, a quality auditor should be familiar with the elements that comprise the system and be able to assess the implementation of these elements. Knowledge of the following elements can also provide readers, whether or not they are quality auditors, with a guideline for implementing a total quality system within their own companies. Familiarizing a company's employees with these elements can provide the company with a basis for a continuous quality improvement program. An understanding of the elements by employees will enable them to bring to management areas of concern regarding compliance.

Endnotes

1. Thresh, *Effective Quality Audits*, 2–12.
2. Ibid.
3. Ibid., 2–5.
4. Ibid., 2–7.

Chapter 7

The First Seven Elements of a Quality System

The next three chapters will describe the basic elements of a total quality system. Based on my experience as a quality assurance coordinator and as a quality auditor, these 21 elements comprise the utopian criterion for a total quality system. They are a composite of the most prominent characteristics from such quality assurance standards as the ANSI/ISO/ASQC Q9000 standards, nuclear specifications, military specifications, and so forth. The appropriate components from nationally and internationally recognized quality assurance standards are incorporated into these elements. For the reader's convenience, these elements are ordered in the same sequence as the ANSI/ISO/ASQC Q9000 standards and include the additional element of quality costs.

It is up to the discretion of management to evaluate the impact these quality elements will have upon its product or service. Management is then responsible for determining the degree to which these quality elements will be incorporated into the quality system.

The following 21 elements are a guideline for establishing a total quality system. All auditors should know what the basic elements are in order to assess the particular elements a company has implemented to comply with generic standards, mutually agreed-upon contractual requirements, and policy statements.

Element 1—Management Responsibility

Management establishes the quality policy and objectives that will be used by the company or organization.

Quality Policy. A quality policy is the directive given by management to a company that defines the statement of principles to be used for quality. The quality policy must be visible. It could be stated through the use of posted corporate policy statements or the corporate policy manual, or carried on cards or in books by individual employees within the company. The corporate quality policy is written in such a manner as to be clearly understood by all members of the organization.

In order for it to be effective, a process must exist for communicating and implementing the corporate policy directives.

Quality Objectives. Management objectives are the desired results of an organization to be achieved within a specified period of time. Management uses quality planning for both long- and short-term improvements. Documentation typically comes in the form of quality business plans or an ancillary list of quality improvement projects used for the planning of implementing quality objectives. In addition to quality planning, management develops a quality plan. A quality plan is defined by the ANSI/ASQC A3-1987 as "a document setting out the specific quality practices, resources, and activities relevant to a particular product, process, service, contract, or project."[1]

To this end, management determines the key elements of the company's quality system. Management identifies where process controls and quality inspection points should be used (quality plan). Product specification criteria are established, and procedures are developed to measure conformance to these standards. In addition, a system to measure the reliability of a product or service is developed to establish conformance and performance criteria.

Management is responsible for developing a cost system for its product or service, as well as a quality cost system that takes into account preventive, appraisal, and failure cost analysis.

Management is responsible for providing a safe working environment.

Quality System. A quality system must be understandable and effective. People, money, and training for continuous improvement are allocated. Prevention should be valued more than detection. The system is set up to satisfy or exceed customer or contractual requirements. Typically, a quality policy manual states how a company plans to comply with the required elements of its quality system.

Review of Quality Management System. At defined intervals, management reviews of the quality system ensure continuing suitability and effectiveness. In the case of the ANSI/ISO/ASQC Q9000 standards, a management representative is required for the implementation of quality standards.

Element 2—Quality System

Structure of the Quality System. The structure of the quality system is established such that the ultimate responsibility for decisions is clearly defined. Delegated authority can be communicated by the use of organizational charts or in a narrative form. The auditor should be familiar with the various types of organizational formats to understand how the system runs. Two examples of organizational structures are military (Figure 7.1) and orthogonal (Figure 7.2). In a military organizational structure, lines of communication flow vertically through existing departments with each department reporting to one lead authority. In this type of organizational setup, individual departments are well-informed of areas in need of improvement. Interaction between departments (horizontal flow of information) may be somewhat lacking, which could lead to a possible obstacle in the implementation of certain processes.

An orthogonal organizational structure is more process- or project-oriented. There is interaction between people from different departments and different fields of expertise who all report to the lead person in charge of the particular process or project communication. It is interactive across the department lines. An example of an orthogonal organizational structure might be found in an advertising firm, where people from the marketing, publishing, writing, and editing departments all contribute their expertise toward the final result.

Recent trends have seen a shift from a strictly military type of organizational structure to a combination of a military and orthogonal structure in an effort to broaden lines of communication.

Along with organizational charts that represent the formal structure of a company, companies may also provide responsibility charts. These charts clearly delineate and identify the positions within each department responsible for various job functions. An example might be a chart that supplies the information of which positions in a particular department are responsible for such tasks as testing of products, calibration of equipment, document control, and so forth.

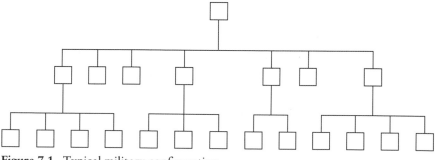

Figure 7.1. Typical military configuration.

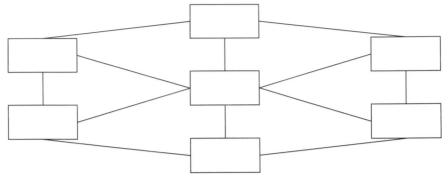

Figure 7.2. Typical orthogonal configuration.

An auditor should be aware of the organizational structure that exists in the facility being audited, as the different lines of communication have an impact upon the TQM system.

Human factors exist that can also affect the quality and performance of a company. Although attitudes are hard to quantify during an audit, some data that can be used are absentee rates, turnover rates, cleanliness of work areas, and an overall negative or positive environment as perceived by the auditor.

The process of acquiring qualified personnel to fill specialized positions is taken into account in the overall quality system, as is an established training system that is planned, implemented, and verified through documentation to ensure that employees are trained and qualified to perform their jobs properly.

Documentation of the Quality System. There is documentation of quality planning for short- and long-term improvements, which includes policy statements, process instructions, procedures, job work instructions, quality projects, and the maintenance of quality records.

Element 3—Contract Review

A process exists to review, define, and document contractual requirements. It assesses the capability to meet contractual requirements. The review ensures that all applicable requirements and any necessary amendments are in compliance and are communicated to the appropriate areas of production or service. Where contractual requirements cannot be met, differences are resolved. These reviews are to be documented and retained.

Element 4—Design Control

A process exists for design control and contains the following elements.

Specification and Design Input. The translation of customer requirements to contractual manufacturing criteria and user needs to production requirements.

Produceability. The knowledge of the manufacturing capabilities of the company and communication of areas of concern between customer and manufacturer.

Design Planning. Defining the responsibilities for manufacturing the item, understanding the technical needs for manufacturing the item, communicating the similarities and differences to other standard products, and knowing the quality requirements (acceptance criteria, statutory requirements, reliability, serviceability, performance criteria, conformance criteria, and methods of disposing of waste products and by-products as necessary).

Design Product Testing and Measurement. Determining the test methods, types of measurements, test frequencies, and equipment to be used.

Design Qualification and Verification. Through the use of nondestructive and destructive methods of evaluation or testing (such as radiography, ultrasound, tensile, and computer simulations), product design can be preapproved, validated, and qualified prior to or during actual production. Evaluations should take into account risk assessment, performance, conformance, and operational conditions.

Design Review and Production Release. At appropriate stages of design and prior to production release, design drawings and specifications may require management approval, customer approval, and verification by appropriate documentation.

Market Readiness Review.

1. The documentation that needs to accompany the product, such as installation manuals, operation manuals, and maintenance manuals
2. Customer service
3. Training of field personnel regarding the new product
4. Availability of spare parts

Design Change Control. If the design needs to be changed, it goes through the same review process and requirements as the original design control process. Controls for obsolete documents are established.

Design Requalification. Reevaluation according to original or new requirements, communication of process modifications, and analysis of feedback regarding conformance and performance of new design changes.

Element 5—Document Control

A process is in place for those documents or electronic media identified by management that require document control. Factors to be taken into consideration are as follows:

1. A process is in place for the generation of documents that includes the writing of the policies and procedures drawings and specifications or other required documentation, approval of the content of the documents, and the distribution of the documents. Examples of the last item are a sign-off area upon receipt of the document, distribution directives at the bottom of the document, or a tally sheet of distribution.

2. Documentation fulfilling the needs of contractual or process requirements is available at all locations in which these functions are performed.

3. A process is in place for the control of revisions to or redistribution of documents using the same system as the original document distribution.

4. A process is in place for the identification and removal of obsolete documents to ensure against unintended use.

Element 6—Procurement

A process is in place for the planning and control of the procurement of supplies and/or services. Attention is given to such things as the type of (long- or short-term) relationship with the supplier, impact on quality, ultimate cost, and the potential cost of the nonconformance of the product/service. The inquiry is shown to potential suppliers to ensure they can meet requirements. Value-added suppliers are sought.

A process is in place for the selection of qualified suppliers. Suppliers need to demonstrate their capability and reliability to meet or exceed product/service requirements. Methods of selection of qualified suppliers can include on-site assessments, evaluation of test samples, past history of product/service performance or conformance data, and published experiences of others who have used the product or service.

Quality assurance criteria are developed between purchaser and supplier. Taken into consideration are records to be submitted, such as test reports verifying the acceptability of chemical or physical properties of products supplied, types of sampling to be used, inspection or verification methods to be used (on-site or receipt), periodic assessments, or assessments as needed.

Purchase orders, which include quality system requirements, product tolerance specifications, quantities, and all other requirements, should be clearly stated. There is a process in place for the review of purchase orders to ensure that they include all stated requirements.

A process is in place for incoming/receiving inspection planning and control. Adequate inspection planning and types of sampling are provided for, whether it be 100 percent inspection or guided by a sampling plan. Characteristics are determined that must be measured and verified so as to meet requirements. A quarantine area exists for items that need further evaluation or do not meet specifications. In some instances, electronic segregation may be used.

A process is in place to resolve quality disputes or noncompliances. Channels of communication are developed that provide for the resolution of quality disputes or nonconformances. Authority figures and contacts at the supplier's facility are known to the purchaser.

A process is in place for receiving, collecting, and retaining quality records. Examples are supplier performance assessments, test reports, trend analysis, identification, and traceability of product and/or process.

Element 7—Customer/Purchaser Supplied Product

A process is in place that provides for verification, inventory, security, storage, maintenance, and the reporting of damaged material of customer-supplied products while still at the supplier's facility.

Endnotes

1. ANSI/ASQC A3-1987, 4.

Chapter 8

The Next Seven Elements
of a Quality System

Element 8—Product Identification and Traceability

Identification and traceability in industry are often thought to mean the same thing; however, there are distinct differences between them. *Product identification* is the present physical marking or written documentation or computerized identification of a product. *Traceability* is the historical progression of events from the start to the finished version of a product.

A process shall be in place that identifies the product from drawings, specifications, documents, or computers throughout the process. Included in this system are procedures that address handling/processing, storage, and identification of quality status (conforming vs. nonconforming via red tags or computer holds). Records of traceability are maintained by such methods as heat number, individual items, lot number, and batch number that enable the raw material to be unquestionably linked to the finished product. In addition, shipment records of items are maintained.

Element 9—Process Control

A process system is in place that controls production to comply with or exceed internal and/or external quality plans or standards. Some factors to consider for establishing a quality plan are

- Standards and codes
- Acceptance standards that include criteria for tolerances and criteria for workmanship
- Status verification—checking for the previously mentioned criteria
- Documented work instructions, specifications, and drawings
- Type of equipment to be used in both the production process and the measurement process

- Process flow diagrams that account for the identification of key variables
- A system to evaluate and measure key variables

Process capabilities are established based on the PDCA cycle.

- Process effectiveness is known.
- Yields of production are known.
- Quality costs, such as dollars spent on prevention, appraisal, and internal and external failure costs, are known.
- Product characteristics are monitored during production and installation.
- Data are reviewed through the use of control charts, histograms, trend analyses, and so forth.
- Systems for controls based on data are reinstituted.

The impact of production on the environment and the impact of the environment on the production is taken into consideration. Some environmental items that should be addressed are the water, the air, type and quantity of power to be used during production, chemical pollution, the impact of temperature and humidity on production, the cleanliness of the production process, the safety of the disposal of the product or its by-products, and regulations in regard to the environment.

Equipment Control and Maintenance.

- Determination of equipment to be used is established prior to use. If needed, approval is attained for the use of this equipment by internal and external authorities.
- There are procedures for preventive maintenance. These can include procedures for the protection of machinery, winterizing machinery, protection from environmental factors, protection against vandalism, protection during lack of use due to shutdowns, and so forth.
- There are qualified personnel to repair equipment. Trend analysis performance of repairs is done.
- Considering computers as part of the equipment, authorized access to the use of the computer is established to prevent unauthorized usage and change or loss of records.

Special Processes.

- The standardization and calibration of equipment is established and maintained.

- According to most standards and regulations, the following items are considered to be in the category of special processes.
    - Welding
    - Brazing
    - Nondestructive testing inspection, such as magnetic particle, ultrasound, X-ray, dye penetrant, visual, electronic, and eddy current
    - Chemical, metallurgical, biological, and radiological processes

- There is verification of qualified personnel to perform special processes and verification of tests performed during special processes.
    - Operator capabilities and qualifications are established.
    - There are certification records for processes, equipment, and personnel.
    - There are records of tests performed that include time, temperature, and other background information; personnel performing tests; validation of test reporting; and filing of results (record retention).

Consideration is given to special processes that need to be performed during the manufacturing process before full assembly is completed or service is delivered. A process should be in place that identifies, documents, and verifies these occurrences.

Workmanship. A process control system is in place that ensures that the workmanship meets product or service criteria.

Element 10—Inspection and Testing

A process is in place for the incoming inspection of a product that utilizes sampling plans that are documented, implemented, and verified. If required, certification is verified and records are retained. Conformance to requirements is verified for both sampling and certification, which allows the product or service to undergo further processing.

A process is in place for in-process inspection, which is also known as *quality checkpoints*. During this process

- Location and frequency are established, planned, documented, and implemented.
- Conformance to requirements is verified. Verifications may occur throughout the process, such as during the use of first piece setup, and permanent or nonpermanent inspection points (random checkpoints) are established.
- Personnel performing inspections are identified, such as production personnel, QA personnel, or third-party personnel.
- There is documentation of personnel responsible for final decisions.

A process is in place for final inspection and testing. During this process

- Acceptance inspection and/or tests are performed. Methods that can be used are 100 percent inspection, lot sampling, continuous sampling, or random sampling.
- The product is audited on a continuous, periodic, or random basis.
- There is feedback concerning nonconformances, both internally and to the customer, if required.

Inspection and Test Records. Records are maintained that provide verification of test and inspection status and identify inspection authority responsible for release.

Element 11—Inspection, Measuring, and Test Equipment

Measurement controls are in place to ensure that there is a high level of confidence in the repeatability of standardized test equipment, standards, and inspection tools. Factors to consider are: written calibration specifications; types of machinery used for calibration; calibration standards used for comparisons; personnel trained in metrology techniques, which involve what tools to use and how and when to use them; devices used for acceptance of product, which include process control tools and final inspection tools; and elements of the environment, such as temperature and humidity.

Standardization/Calibration Controls. Standardization is the ability of a piece of equipment to produce similar results each time it is used and may include external adjustments of the equipment to conform to known standards. The extent to which such standards are documented is left to the discretion of the management of the company being audited. Calibration is a formal system of standardization and may require internal adjustments of the machine to conform to industrial or recognized national standards, such as provided by the National Institute of Standards and Technology (NIST). Both standardization and calibration take into consideration the precision, usage, and durability of the equipment. For example, the environment may be harsh, as in a steel mill, so the equipment needs to be more durable. Sometimes, when durability is increased, precision is decreased.

To have a good calibration/standardization program, there should be written procedures and work instructions covering such items as how to calibrate, frequency of calibration, and how to measure. Documented evidence of calibrations must exist. Calibration standards must be traceable to nationally or internationally recognized standards. Where no such standards exist, the basis used for calibration is documented. Measurement tools used in the acceptance of product may need to be identified on inspection reports and be traceable back to nationally recognized standards. Trend analysis of calibrated instruments is necessary for reliability of gauges or tools used. If gauges are found to be out of tolerance, corrective actions pertaining to the gauges are implemented and a system is established for the reevaluation of products monitored by those gauges. Where purchase of calibration services is required, the organization is accredited.

A process is in place for records retention of calibrations, standardization, procedures, and work instructions. There is a timetable established for records retention.

Element 12—Inspection and Test Status

There is a process in place that establishes, by suitable means, the status of items covered in Element 10—Inspection and Testing. Records of inspection and testing status are verified by such means as the use of paper records, computer records, product tags, bar codes, and traceability of product with releases. Those personnel responsible for decisions regarding inspection status shall be indicated on inspection status reports as required.

Element 13—Control of Nonconforming Product

If a product is found to be nonconforming, it is identified through such means as a marking, tagging, or computer identification. The nonconforming product is physically or electronically segregated to prevent inadvertent use. Written or computerized records are maintained.

Disposition. A system is in place for the disposition of nonconforming products. There is an evaluation of the status of the nonconforming product by authorized personnel. Status classifications could include whether the product was repaired, reapplied, recalled, referred, or scrapped. If the product required rework or reapplication, then a reevaluation and reclassification against standards of application is done. Documentation for the status of these items exists and may include forms, reports, approvals, waivers, and referrals to the customer.

Element 14—Corrective and Preventive Action

There is a process in place that identifies types of problems that occur from common or special circumstances. The problem is analyzed to determine the root cause and to prevent repetition of the problem. The impact of the problem is evaluated in terms of costs, performance, safety, and customer satisfaction.

Implementing corrective action takes into account the need for a short-term or remedial fix plus long-term actions and the changes required in the process, product, specifications, quality systems, and work instructions. There are designated personnel responsible for the follow-up. There is documentation of the changes made to prevent recurrence. There is an evaluation of the changes made to analyze the effectiveness of the corrective action.

There is a process in place for the initiation of preventive action. Preventive actions that are implemented are evaluated on an ongoing basis to ensure effectiveness.

Chapter 9

The Final Seven Elements
of a Quality System

Element 15—Handling, Storage, Packaging, Preservation, and Delivery

There is a process in place for the handling, storage, packaging, and delivery of goods. Procedures and/or specifications for handling, storage, packaging, and delivery are documented. The process for handling goods and products includes the prevention of damage, the prevention of deterioration or preservation of goods, and the maintenance of identification. There is a secure storage area that prevents deterioration (preservation), provides product identification and traceability, and provides for product locations. Packaging methods prevent damage, maintain identification, and conform to specified requirements. The delivery aspect provides for the protection of the quality of the product after final inspection and includes in-house delivery from area to area and during loading. It also may include transportation to final destination. There is a feedback system for goods that are damaged upon receipt.

Element 16—Quality Records

As it pertains to quality auditing, there is often confusion about the definition of quality records. To eliminate some of the confusion, management needs to define and identify those records it deems appropriate to categorize as quality records. Examples of such quality records are: procedures; production criteria; test data; qualification data and records; process control data and records; audit reports; performance data and records; and calibration data and records.

Quality records are clearly identified. They are traceable to product or process. They are dated and contain the names of personnel responsible for the data collection, including the time, turn, or shift, if necessary. There is a collection process that defines how the data will be collected and which personnel are responsible for collecting them. There is a procedure for indexing quality records that provides for a process of recall (records are retrievable), a specified period of retention, and a specified time of disposal of records. Records are stored in such places as file cabinets, microfiche, and computer disks. The storage environment is selected so as to prevent loss or damage by water, fire, humidity, and so on. Records are securely stored and maintained with personnel designated as responsible for input and maintenance of files. Computerized systems must be safeguarded to prevent unauthorized access to records.

Element 17—Internal Quality Audits

The internal quality audit function includes the scheduling of audits (such as the frequency of audits based on status and importance); audit dates and times; and the scope of the audits as to location, elements being audited, and audit team personnel. Procedures are established, checklists are generated, and auditors undergo a training program. After the implementation of the audit, which is the on-site evaluation, the reporting takes place according to the established levels of informal and formal reporting. The closure phase then takes place, which includes such things as evaluation of corrective action plans, verification of the implementation of corrective actions, and follow-up.

Element 18—Training of Personnel

Training needs are identified and planned with support from the executive level and various other levels of the organization. Qualifications of management, administrative, and technical personnel are determined. Certification may be necessary for specific employees. Certification can occur on various levels, such as internal certification by the company, or by nationally recognized certification organizations, such as welding organizations or medical organizations.

The company provides for the training of personnel to meet business objectives. Training locations and times are determined and may come in the form of classroom lessons or on-the-job experience. There is verification of trained/certified employees based upon their education, training, and experience. Trained employees are evaluated through the use of demonstrated skills. Records of training are maintained, and recertification or requalification is performed.

Human factors are taken into consideration by an auditor. Auditors look for the training of personnel to inspire the desire for continuous quality improvement. Understanding the importance of quality and quality techniques promotes quality awareness, which is the understanding of the individuals' responsibility toward the company and the individuals' impact to product or service performance.

Element 19—Servicing

A process is in place that provides for the servicing of products or services to meet specified requirements. A process for servicing is in place that provides for assembly instructions, additional/spare parts lists, and service numbers. There is a final check to ensure that all auxiliary items are included in the final shipment of the item. There are instructions for the usage and maintenance of the product.

There is liability on the part of the organization to be able to recall records, designs, specifications, process controls, results of testing, and review of other materials involved. There is a system to accommodate claims and traceability for recall.

Safety measures are documented by warning labels, material safety data sheets, and so on. Safety factors include both direct usage of product and indirect usage of product by means of combination with or exposure to other products or environmental conditions that may create a safety concern.

Element 20—Statistical and Analytical Techniques

TQM systems currently emphasize the use of statistical and analytical techniques. Therefore, auditors should become familiar with statistical and analytical techniques used to monitor processes and production. Among the most notable of these process control techniques are flowcharts, control charts (p, np, c, u), trend charts, histograms, Pareto charts, cause/effect diagrams, design of experiments, analysis of variance, tests of significance, and inspection plans/quality levels.

Assessment tools are used that provide the organization with information on how to best apply its product or service, both internally and externally. Examples include market analysis, product design, durability predictions, data analysis (performance assessment, defect analysis), benchmarking, failure mode effect analysis, and quality functions deployment.

Element 21—Quality Costs Analysis

Quality costs are included as an element of a total quality system, as many companies use quality costs and standard costs to evaluate where opportunities for continuous improvement and product costs reside. There are various formats used to monitor quality costs. Some of these formats are as follows.

Standard Cost Format. A standard cost format analyzes the standard cost to produce a particular item versus the actual cost of the production of that item.

Cost of Nonconformance Format. A cost of nonconformance format analyzes the value lost to the company due to the nonconformance. This system may stand alone or be incorporated into a standard cost system.

Quality Costs Format. A quality cost format is a cost accounting process that categorizes either existing or new accounting systems into a format that managers can use to evaluate the quality improvement process. This strengthens the relationship between quality control and quality economics and gives a company an added business value and perhaps a competitive edge in the marketplace. There are four categories within a quality cost format.

1. *Prevention costs.* The costs of all activities specifically designed to prevent poor quality in products or services. Examples include the cost of new product review, quality planning, supplier capability, surveys, process capability evaluations, quality improvement team meetings, quality improvement projects, and quality education and training.

2. *Appraisal costs.* The costs associated with measuring, evaluating, or auditing products or services to ensure conformance to quality standards and performance requirements. These include the costs of incoming and source inspection/test of purchased material; in-process and final inspection/test, product, process, or service audits; calibration of measuring and test equipment; and the cost of associated supplies and materials.

3. *Internal failure costs.* Failure costs occurring prior to delivery or shipment of the product or the furnishing of a service to the customer. Examples include the costs of scrap, rework, reinspection, retesting, material review, and downgrading.

4. *External failure costs.* Failure costs occurring after delivery or shipment of the product and during or after furnishing of a service to the customer. Examples include the costs of processing customer complaints, customer returns, warranty claims, and product recalls.

Additional information about quality cost systems can be found in Appendix B, which contains a detailed description of a quality cost system, excerpted from *Principles of Quality Costs, Second Edition.*

Chapter 10

Statistical Process Control

As part of the continuous quality improvement effort, many companies utilize statistical process control (SPC) techniques as a means of monitoring and controlling variation in their processes. Therefore, quality auditors should become acquainted with these SPC techniques in order to evaluate the validity of their usage in the companies being audited. SPC techniques may be used to discover those out-of-control areas that call for action, to identify and correct causes of bad quality, and to discover those out-of-control areas that indicate relaxed inspection standards.[1]

This chapter provides a brief summary of the most commonly used methods in the SPC arena. Formulas for the calculations used in control charting can be found in Appendix A. For a more comprehensive understanding of statistical methods, further reading is recommended. The Bibliography contains the titles of some of the other books available on this subject.

Identification of Key Process and Product Variables

All products contain specific characteristics that must meet customers' needs. At each step in the production process, provisions should be made to ensure that the desired characteristics are met. This requires identifying the factors in the production process that impact product characteristics. These factors are typically called *key process variables*. Product characteristics of interest are measured at interim points in the production process. Identification of key process and product variables is the first step in setting up a statistical process control system (SPCS). Often, a process map or flowchart is developed to identify and document processing and inspection areas (quality control points) during the production of a product or a service (see Figure 10.1). This map also identifies the process and product measurements taken during the manufacture or delivery of the product or service. A numbering system on the process map is sometimes used to identify standard operating procedures that control the respective process variables. The process map should be evaluated to ensure that the customers' specifications and needs are met and that adequate control points are designed into the process.

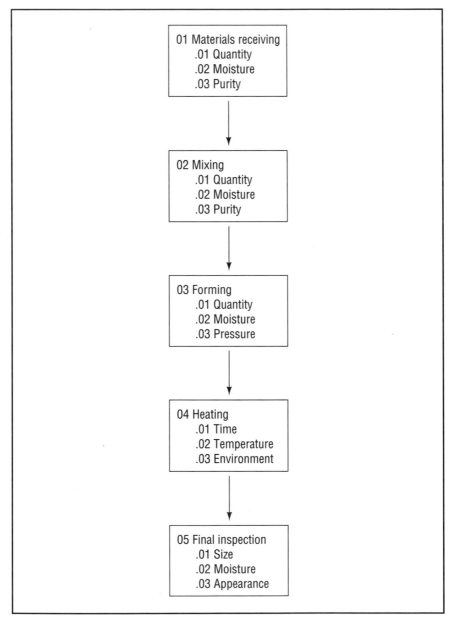

Figure 10.1. Process map or flowchart.

Variability of Processes and Products

Variation in output is the natural state of processes without intervention from external forces. However, since variability is also inherent in the inputs of the process, the output of the process will also vary according to the inputs. It is often convenient to classify the sources of variability into five groups based on the process inputs of human resources, machines, methods, materials, and the environment. The following table can be used to help classify the input factors of product variability and their potential sources.

Input factors of variation	*Examples of potential sources*
Human resources	Training, experience, physical and mental ability, morale, attitude, fatigue
Machines	Component parts, preventive maintenance, parts inventory, wear, age, repairs, vintage, technology
Methods	Procedures, compliance to procedures, controls, measurements, auditing, techniques
Materials	Composition, storage, compliance to specifications, suppliers
Environment	Indoor, outdoor, humidity, temperature, sunshine, rain, atmosphere

The development of the potential sources of variability and the classification into these groups may require a cross-functional team usually selected from the operations, operations management, engineering, and inspection functions.

For each source of variability there are usually several potential and actual causes of variation that will require evaluation. The type of corrective action necessary depends on whether a special or common cause of variation is present. A special cause of variation is a specific condition that can be identified and corrected. The existence of special causes of variation was first explored by Shewhart, who named them *assignable causes*. Examples of special causes of variation are a *specific* employee who is not properly trained or a *specific* machine that needs to be repaired. A common cause of variation is a condition that stems from the general system and impacts the process. For example, all personnel could be affected by the lack of an operator training program. The lack of training is common to all operators. All machines could be affected by the lack of a preventive maintenance/inspection system for equipment. The lack of preventive maintenance would then be a common cause that affects all the machines. Deming adapted Shewhart's ideas and further explored their influence on product quality.[2]

The following table delineates the difference between *special* and *common* causes of variation.

Human resources	Special cause—an operator not trained properly
	Common cause—the absence of an operator training program
Machines	Special cause—a bearing is worn
	Common cause—the absence of a bearing inspection program
Methods	Special cause—operator did not follow procedure
	Common cause—procedure does not exist for doing the job
Materials	Special cause—poor quality material was approved by incoming inspection
	Common cause—the absence of an incoming inspection system
Environment	Special cause—rain increased the moisture content of raw materials
	Common cause—materials are not stored in a controlled environment

Many times, special causes of variation can be detected and corrected at the process level by employee (local) action. For this reason, some authors refer to special causes as *local causes*; however, common causes of variation typically should be resolved by the management system (operations management, engineering, product and process design). Since common causes must be addressed by the management system, they are also referred to as *system causes*. The challenge for management is to determine whether a special or a common cause is present, so that the appropriate functions can be assigned to take action. Often, management assumes that a special cause is present and places much of the blame on the personnel present when a poor quality product is produced. The statistical control chart, first developed by Shewhart, is a tool for both managers and employees to help identify the presence of a special or common cause.

Statistical Control Charts and Process Stability

For any measurement of key process and product variables, statistical limits can be calculated. If the process has not changed from its original condition, a specified large percentage of the subsequent readings would be expected to fall between these limits. If the process has changed from its original condition, the subsequent measurements could be expected to exceed these limits or result in some other recognizable pattern. In a SPCS, the subsequent readings that are within the statistical control limits (based on past data) are assumed to be affected by the same common causes that were in effect when the original data were collected. This is known as *being in statistical control*. When there is statistical control, predictability and stability of a process becomes more readily determined. It is also referred to as *having a stable process*. Data outside the control limits or exhibiting a particular pattern are assumed to be caused by special causes. Finding special causes of variation by using statistical limits is a major tool for identifying process changes. When a point is beyond the limits, it is a signal for all functions involved to check the process and find and eliminate the special cause.

Control Limits and Control Charting Risk

In common practice, the statistical control limits are set to include 99.73 percent of the historical readings charted. The readings that are charted could be measurements from individual units, but they are more commonly an average measurement from a sample of several product units. Because sample averages are less variable than individual data points, statistical limits for sample averages are not as wide as statistical limits for individual points. A common mistake in control charting is to plot individual data points on a control chart whose statistical control limits were based upon the sample averages (such as plotting individual data points on an $\bar{X}$ chart). One could be misled to assume that an out-of-control condition exists because individual data points reside beyond the control limits.

The risks associated with judging statistical control or stability are considered in any decision regarding the acceptability of the product or service. Based on our sample, what we perceive to be happening is compared to the actual condition of our process. The four possibilities are listed in Figure 10.2.

Types of Data Collection

Key process variables can be monitored using two basic types of data: variables (measurement) or attributes (count). Variables (measurement) data are gathered by using actual measurements from measurement instruments. Examples include the weight of materials received being measured in pounds by using a scale; the temperature of the furnace being measured with a pyrometer in degrees (Fahrenheit or Celsius); and the dimensions of the final product are being measured with a micrometer and expressed in thousandths of inches. Variables data are also termed *continuous data*. With the use of a more accurate measurement instrument to measure the same object, a slightly different result could be expected. For example, a scale that measures to the nearest pound might record an object's weight as 20 pounds, whereas

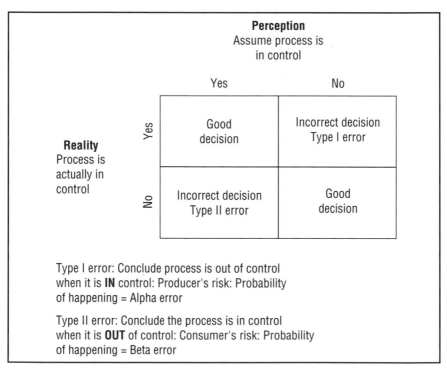

Figure 10.2. Risks associated with control charting.

a scale that measures to the tenths of a pound might record the same object as weighing 19.6 pounds. Furthermore, a scale that measures to the hundredths of a pound might record the same object as weighing 19.57 pounds. Taking this to an extreme, the object's "true" weight may be 19.571627345 pounds. With variable or continuous data, values that reside within each increment of measurement could be interpreted as the possible "true" value of the measurement and depend upon the accuracy (measurement increment) of the measurement instrument used. Auditors evaluating variables data should be aware of the types of measurement tools used and their proper applications to ensure that the results of such measurements are accurate. Managerial decisions are based on the results of the data collected, and managerial decisions can be only as good as the accuracy of the data.

Attributes (count data) are generated by counting the number of times an attribute of interest occurs. Attributes data are also referred to as *discrete data* because a unit of product must fall into one of several discrete categories. For example, two of the last 50 articles inspected failed the go/no-go gauge for dimensional inspection. In this example, a part falls into either the conforming category or the nonconforming category. For a given lot of 50, one unit could be nonconforming or two units could be nonconforming, but 1.5 units could not be nonconforming. Another example is to count the number of snags on a sample of cloth inspected. In any given sample, there could be two snags or three snags, but not 2.4 snags. Knowing the type of data collected is important, because different types of control charts are used for each type of data.

Control Charts for Variables

The most common types of control charts for variables (measurement) data are the $\bar{x}$ (pronounced X-bar) control chart and the R control chart. The $\bar{x}$ control chart illustrates the average measurement of the samples taken over time. The R control chart illustrates the range of the measurements of the samples taken.

When setting up $\bar{x}$ and R control charts, it is critical that the individual items that comprise the sample are pulled from the same basic production process. The samples should be pulled at about the same time, from the same machine, from the same raw material source, and so on. This may require separate control charts for each machine or for each source of variation. It is especially important to keep potentially unlike data separate when setting up a control chart and establishing control limits. Sources of variation should be identified through brainstorming sessions before charting begins. The process of segregating data to be charted by potential sources of variation is often called *rational subgrouping*.

Samples are pulled in groups, with each group containing a specified amount of sample items that usually range from two to 10. The $\bar{x}$ control chart plots the sample mean (average of samples) of each sample group over time. The sample mean indicates the current performance level of the key process variable. For example, if the average measurement of five consecutive items in one sample group is 6.997 inches, one would conclude that the current process performance is near 6.997 inches. Under normal conditions, it can be assumed that the sample mean will be close to the process mean at the time the process samples were taken.

The grand average, $\bar{\bar{x}}$ (pronounced X-double bar), indicates the average of all the sample means ($\bar{x}$). A solid line drawn at the arithmetic center of the $\bar{x}$ grid represents the grand average $\bar{\bar{x}}$.

The R control chart plots the range value for each sample group. The range value is determined by subtracting the lowest measurement from the highest measurement in a given sample group. The range value indicates the variability in the process. The larger the range value, the larger the variation in the process.

Figure 10.3 shows an example of an $\bar{x}$ and R control chart. The header contains general information about the process, including the machine used, the part inspected, the operator responsible for the chart, the measurement, and so forth. The data portion contains the individual measurements that make up the sample and the calculated values of $\bar{x}$ and R. The chart portion contains two grids on which to plot the sample averages and ranges. The upper control limit (UCL) and lower control limit (LCL) are calculated for both the $\bar{x}$ and the R charts. Typically, these limits are represented on these charts by dashed lines. If the process has not changed from the historic period from which the UCL and LCL were calculated, virtually all (99.73 percent) of the subsequent values of $\bar{x}$ and R should be within these limits.

If certain patterns exist on the control chart, one can conclude that special causes of variation are at work in the process. Auditors should be aware of these patterns on control charts, which indicate out-of-control conditions. They then need to verify that managerial actions have been taken to determine the root cause of these out-of-control points and verify that corrective actions have been taken to eliminate these conditions. Figures 10.4 through 10.8 identify specific signals on the control chart that show typical out-of-control conditions. Other

Variables Control Chart
Form 190 (Rev 8)

① Bad inserts

Product			Plant Division and or Quality Products Division			Measurement Diameter	Chart no
RS 4428B						Spec Ref Drawing A/070 Rev. 2	

Recorder		Specific Operation Drill 578		Specification limits 7± 60 mm	Zero equals
Machine Operator		Measuring device (including serial no) Serial # 430		Unit of measure	

Date			9/1/94									9/1/94						9/1/94						9/2/94		
Time		7am	8	9	10	11	12n	1pm	2	3	4	5	6	7am	8	9	10	11	12n	1pm	2	3	4	5	6	
Sample measurements	1	7.6	7.3	7.1	6.7	7.0	6.6	7.2	6.6	6.6	6.5	6.5	6.7	6.4	6.9	7.4	6.4	7.0	6.8	6.5	6.7	6.5	6.9	6.7	
	2	6.9	7.5	6.8	7.0	7.2	6.3	7.1	7.3	7.3	6.9	7.4	6.9	6.3	7.1	7.1	6.6	7.0	7.2	7.3	6.9	6.8	7.4	7.1	
	3	7.4	6.4	7.3	6.7	7.4	7.4	7.3	6.7	6.7	7.7	6.7	7.9	6.4	7.7	7.6	6.6	7.1	7.6	7.3	7.7	7.3	7.4	7.0	
	4	7.1	7.3	7.6	5.9	7.2	8.5	6.7	6.9	7.3	7.3	7.3	7.0	6.2	7.2	6.8	6.9	6.7	7.4	6.4	7.0	6.4	7.3	6.4	
	5	7.4	7.1	7.2	6.6	7.5	7.1	6.7	7.9	7.9	6.9	6.8	6.7	6.1	6.4	6.9	7.2	6.5	6.2	6.9	6.8	6.9	7.6	6.8	
Sum		36.4	35.6	35.0	32.9	36.3	35.9	35.0	35.4	35.4	35.3	34.7	35.2	31.4	35.3	35.8	33.7	34.3	35.2	34.3	35.2	34.7	35.8	34.3	
Average X̄		7.3	7.1	7.2	6.6	7.3	7.2	7.0	7.1	7.1	7.1	6.9	7.0	6.3	7.1	7.2	6.7	6.9	7.0	6.9	7.0	6.9	7.2	6.9	
Range R		.7	1.1	.8	1.1	.5	2.2	.6	1.3	1.3	1.2	.9	1.2	.3	1.3	.8	.8	.6	1.4	.9	1.3	.9	.9	.7	
Notes												①													

UCL_X̄ = 7.64 — 7.6
X̄ = 7.04 — 7.0
LCL_X̄ = 6.44 — 6.4

Averages

UCL_R = 2.20 — 3.0 / 2.0
R̄ = 1.00 — 1.0
LCL_R

Ranges

Figure 10.3. Sample x̄ and R chart.

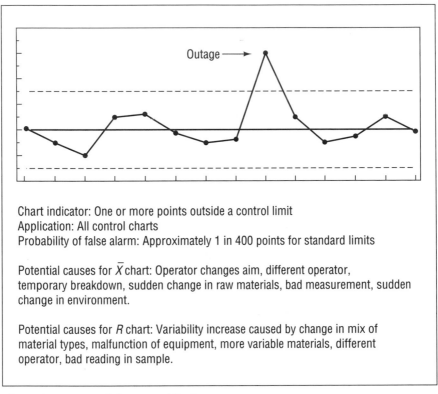

Chart indicator: One or more points outside a control limit
Application: All control charts
Probability of false alarm: Approximately 1 in 400 points for standard limits

Potential causes for $\bar{X}$ chart: Operator changes aim, different operator, temporary breakdown, sudden change in raw materials, bad measurement, sudden change in environment.

Potential causes for R chart: Variability increase caused by change in mix of material types, malfunction of equipment, more variable materials, different operator, bad reading in sample.

Figure 10.4. Beyond the control limits or outage.

statistical books should be referenced to provide the auditor with additional information pertaining to out-of-control scenarios.

Control Charts for Attributes (Count) Data

Control charts for attributes data have some similarities to control charts for variables. Samples are taken periodically, and the results of many samples are charted over time. As with variables control charts, the samples should come from logical subgroups. Typically, since variables data give more precise information, fewer samples need to be pulled in order to avoid alpha and beta type errors. While it generally takes less time to measure the pulled samples for attributes data, however, more samples should be taken to avoid alpha and beta type errors. Control is judged by whether the new samples pulled are similar to the historical period from which control limits were established.

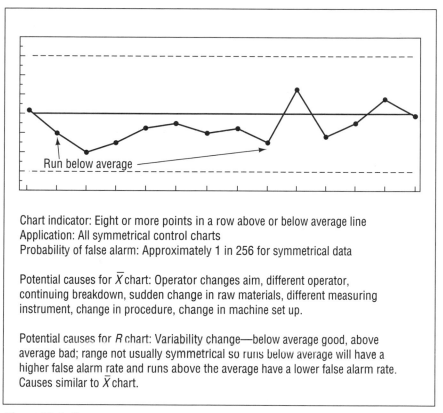

Chart indicator: Eight or more points in a row above or below average line
Application: All symmetrical control charts
Probability of false alarm: Approximately 1 in 256 for symmetrical data

Potential causes for $\bar{X}$ chart: Operator changes aim, different operator, continuing breakdown, sudden change in raw materials, different measuring instrument, change in procedure, change in machine set up.

Potential causes for R chart: Variability change—below average good, above average bad; range not usually symmetrical so runs below average will have a higher false alarm rate and runs above the average have a lower false alarm rate. Causes similar to $\bar{X}$ chart.

Figure 10.5. Runs.

The out-of-control conditions illustrated in the variable or measurement data section generally apply to attributes charts also. With attribute data, however, if the sample size is small, the data charted may not be symmetric. Under this condition, the procedures used for calculating control limits in Appendix A are not recommended.

There are several basic types of control charts that can be used for charting attributes data. Attributes data count either the number of nonconforming product units that fail to conform to one or more specifications, or the number of each occurrence of nonconformity contained in the product units.

To chart nonconforming product units, the p-chart or np-chart is used. In the p-chart, the fraction rejected, p, is defined as the ratio of number of nonconforming product units found in an inspection or

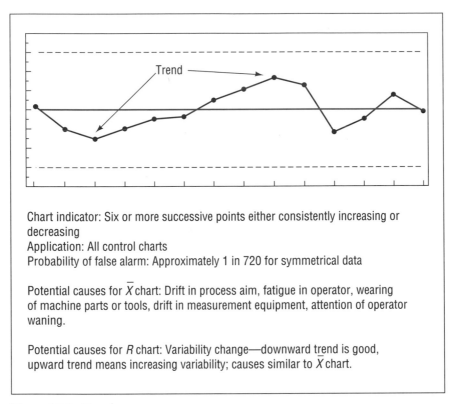

Chart indicator: Six or more successive points either consistently increasing or decreasing
Application: All control charts
Probability of false alarm: Approximately 1 in 720 for symmetrical data

Potential causes for $\bar{X}$ chart: Drift in process aim, fatigue in operator, wearing of machine parts or tools, drift in measurement equipment, attention of operator waning.

Potential causes for R chart: Variability change—downward trend is good, upward trend means increasing variability; causes similar to $\bar{X}$ chart.

Figure 10.6. Trends.

series of inspections to the number of product units inspected.[3] This is typically expressed and plotted in terms of a proportion.

The np-chart is used to plot nonconforming units in a subgroup to determine the quantity of nonconforming units where the data are collected using constant sample sizes. The np-chart plots the output of a process as the actual number of nonconforming product units in the subgroup being inspected.

The c-chart plots the number of nonconformities contained in a sampling subgroup. The application of a c-chart is not only to show that a product unit is defective, but also to show how many nonconformities the product unit has. A c-chart becomes a plot of the number of nonconformities contained in a subgroup of constant sample size.

The u-chart is similar to a c-chart, except that the plotted data represent the number of nonconformances per *unit* in a subgroup, instead of just the number of nonconformities of that subgroup. When subgroups

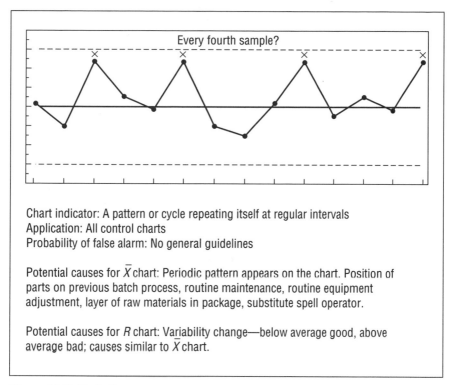

Chart indicator: A pattern or cycle repeating itself at regular intervals
Application: All control charts
Probability of false alarm: No general guidelines

Potential causes for $\overline{X}$ chart: Periodic pattern appears on the chart. Position of parts on previous batch process, routine maintenance, routine equipment adjustment, layer of raw materials in package, substitute spell operator.

Potential causes for R chart: Variability change—below average good, above average bad; causes similar to $\overline{X}$ chart.

Figure 10.7. Periodic.

do not contain constant sample sizes, a u-chart should be used as opposed to a c-chart.

In summary, the following categories of control charts are used for attributes data.

p-chart—The ratio of nonconforming product units to the number of product units inspected.

np-chart—The actual number of nonconforming product units compared to the product units inspected (subgroups are of constant sample size).

c-chart—The number of nonconformities contained in a subgroup of constant sample size.

u-chart—The number of nonconformities per unit in a subgroup of varying sample size. This is expressed in terms of a proportion.

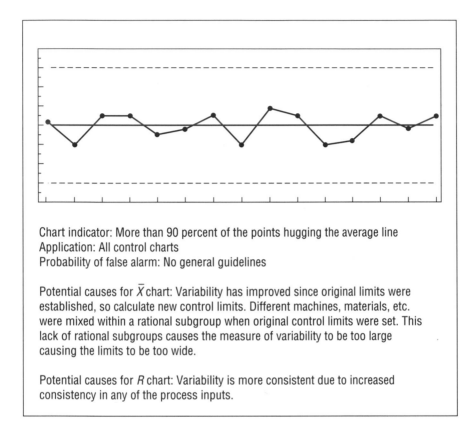

Chart indicator: More than 90 percent of the points hugging the average line
Application: All control charts
Probability of false alarm: No general guidelines

Potential causes for $\bar{X}$ chart: Variability has improved since original limits were established, so calculate new control limits. Different machines, materials, etc. were mixed within a rational subgroup when original control limits were set. This lack of rational subgroups causes the measure of variability to be too large causing the limits to be too wide.

Potential causes for R chart: Variability is more consistent due to increased consistency in any of the process inputs.

Figure 10.8. Stratification.

Endnotes

1. Grant and Leavenworth, *Statistical Quality Control*, 234.

2. Deming, *Out of the Crisis*, 310–12.

3. Grant and Leavenworth, *Statistical Quality Control*, 223.

Chapter 11

Statistical Sampling for Auditing

This chapter provides quality auditors with a hands-on application of simple sampling techniques particular to the quality auditing field. Sampling is a method of obtaining information that estimates the value or quality of a population by examining only a part of the total population when a particular process or product of a quality system is being evaluated. Financial auditors have long had the luxury of using statistical sampling analysis when performing audits. In general, they are zeroing in on a particular aspect of a quality accounting system, so statistical sampling can be readily used. Using the proper sampling techniques for the numerous elements involved in a quality system audit would be a laborious and time-consuming task. This chapter is dedicated to a few of the sampling techniques that quality auditors can use if statistical evaluations are deemed practical by the auditor in auditing a particular quality element process or product.

Sampling is part common sense and part scientific principles. It is important that quality auditors use their judgment and common sense in the application of these statistical methods during the performance of a system audit. Their usage may be more appropriate to process, compliance, and product audits.

Statistical sampling uses results to project the condition of a field that has been examined with a stated reliability. While there is no universal sampling method that will achieve the objective of all possible audit evaluations, there are a variety of approaches to sampling available. Three popular techniques that will be explored here are estimation sampling, acceptance sampling, and discovery or exploratory sampling.

Estimation Sampling

Estimation sampling provides the answer to the question of how many or how much. In this method, a random sample of a specific size is obtained and the number of specified nonconformances is counted. Estimation sampling provides the auditor with an estimate of the frequency of occurrences of an event in the field. In addition, it considers the interval range of the sampling error, which is called a *precision* or a *point estimate*. Error rates must be estimated because population variability has an effect on the sample size. The larger the nonconformance rate, the larger the variability, and, therefore, a larger sample size is needed to accomplish the same precision. This must be considered when relying on the sample result. "The sampling error is a statement of how far from the value obtainable from a 100 percent check the sample result might be."[1] These statements hold true until a nonconformance rate of 50 percent is reached. Once the nonconformance rate exceeds 50 percent, the necessary sample size begins to decrease. If the rate of nonconformance exceeds 50 percent, the auditor and the auditee would have more to be concerned with than the proper sample size. Therefore, the tables in Appendix D do not include sample sizes for nonconformance rates greater than 50 percent. In reality, management should be investigating conditions when nonconformance rates are substantially lower than 50 percent.

The process of determining sample size requires considerable thought and judgment on the part of the auditor. Attention must be given to the desired sample precision necessary to estimate the characteristics under evaluation. A decision must also be made regarding the probability of assurance of making the correct decision based on the sample taken (confidence level).

Desired sample precision is based on the risk and consequences of making an error. Statistical sampling tests indicating relatively large sample precision ranges may be acceptable in some instances, such as a 10 percent to 15 percent precision range in estimating inventory balances; however, a precision range as low as 1 percent of a statistical sample might be considered intolerable because of the impact of the particular characteristic under evaluation (such as the failure rates of airplane engines). It is the auditor's responsibility to determine the confidence level of making the right decision based on the sample. The higher the confidence level (the lower the risk of being wrong), the larger the required sample size.

Appendix D contains the tables for estimating sample size—attributes reprinted from Herbert Arkin's *Handbook of Sampling for Auditing and Accounting*. The formulas for the derivations of tables generated in Appendix D can be found on pages 75–99 of Arkin's book. For the auditor's convenience, the range of confidence and precision levels most commonly used have been included in Appendix D.

Note that percentage numbers expressed in the tables are stated in absolute terms. As an example, if the true population value is 6 percent and the precision is ±2 percent, the sample value would be expected to be in the range of 4 percent to 8 percent, *not* 6 percent ± (2 percent of 6 percent) or 6 percent ± 0.12 percent.

Steps to Determine Appropriate Sample Size Using Appendix D

1. Establish the required sample precision (±1 percent, ±2 percent, and so on).

2. Establish the desired confidence level (90 percent, 95 percent, and so on).

3. Estimate the maximum expected rate of occurrence.

4. Determine the approximate field size.

5. Refer to the sample size table (Appendix D).[2] These tables are based on two-sided normal distribution curves.

   a. Select the maximum expected occurrence rate level.

   b. Select the section of the table for the desired confidence level.

   c. Find the row for the field (population) size.

   d. Find the column for the desired sample precision.

   e. The sample size to be taken is at the intersection of the column and row.

Example Using Appendix D Tables

The expected rate of occurrence is not to be over 5 percent. The confidence level desired is being 90 percent assured of coming to the right conclusion (assessment of nonconformance rate). The desired precision is ±2 percent. The field size is 1000. Turn to Table D.1b. Look at 1000 for field size (population size). Move across to the intersection at ±2 percent precision column. The sample size to be taken is 244.

Using this example in estimation sampling, with a range of precision from ±2 percent to ±4 percent, the amount of samples needed is reduced from 244 to 75. Observe from this example that, as we use a wider range of precision, we need to take fewer samples.

Acceptance Sampling

Acceptance sampling is when an acceptable quality level is determined and a certain number of samples are taken, depending on the lot size. If the amount of rejectable conditions found in the samples taken do not exceed a predetermined number, the lot is considered acceptable. If the samples taken contain rejectable conditions that exceed a predetermined level, parameters concerning retesting or rejecting the lot are stated in the standards. For further elaboration on this type of sampling, the military specification, MIL-STD-105E or MIL-STD-414 is recommended.

In the case of acceptance sampling, most, if not all, of the following parameters are known: process capabilities, nonconformance rate, acceptable quality levels, universe size, and lot size. Typically, however, the quality auditor does not have the luxury of knowing these parameters, and, in particular, the continuous production of lots is not available. In addition, some areas may be audited where acceptable quality levels have not been determined. Therefore, this book will not detail acceptance sampling and the use of MIL-STD-105E and MIL-STD-414, as they are not recommended for use on quality audits.

Acceptance sampling provides an accept-reject decision. It does not indicate the rate of occurrence of nonconformance.

Discovery Sampling

Discovery or exploratory sampling is a fastidious method of sampling, as it is used to disclose even one nonconformance within a given field size. It discloses a needle-in-a-haystack type of situation, such as one instance of nonconformance in two million entries.[3] Discovery sampling is a plan that provides assurance of a prescribed confidence level of finding at least one nonconforming condition in a particular lot and, therefore, is a preferred method when performing internal audits to disclose inadvertent clerical or arithmetical errors or to disclose manipulation or fraud. Discovery sampling should not be used to determine the percentage of occurrence or the frequency of occurrence, but rather to find at least a single occurrence of that type of nonconformance. The purpose of discovery sampling is disclosure, not acceptance or rejection of items under investigation.[4]

Steps to Determine Appropriate Sample Size
Using Appendix E

The formulas for the derivations of tables generated in Appendix E can be found on pages 132–140 in Herbert Arkin's *Handbook of Sampling for Auditing and Accounting*. The tables provided in Appendix E are stated probability levels of 85 percent, 90 percent, 95 percent, and 99 percent of discovering a single nonconformance when the occurrence rate is proportionate to 0.1 to 5 with field sizes ranging from 200 to 50,000.

1. Establish the probability level required.

2. Estimate the occurrence rate.

3. Determine the approximate field size.

4. Refer to Appendix E tables.

   a. Select the proper probability table.

   b. Find the row for the field size.

   c. Find the column for the occurrence rate.

   d. The sample size to be taken is at the intersection of the row and column.

Example Using Appendix E Tables

The desired probability level is 90 percent. The field size is 1000. The occurrence rate is 5.0 percent. (Although not specifically indicated on the tables in Appendix E, the numbers of occurrence rates are expressed in terms of percentages.) Turn to the table with a probability level of 90 percent. Look at 1000 for field size (population size). Move across to the intersection at occurrence rate 5.0 percent column. The sample size to be taken is 45.

Additional tables of probability for use in discovery (exploratory) sampling where discovery of nonconformances is greater than one can be found in *Tables of Probability for Use in Exploratory Sampling*, published by the office of the Auditor General, Department of the U.S. Air Force. Additional tables can also be found in *Sawyer's Internal Auditing* by Lawrence B. Sawyer.

Sample Selection

In planning the sample selection, the auditor needs to determine

- Critical items or key elements of process variables and process controls
- Critical work instructions
- Highly stressed, high-volume, or high-precision areas
- Contributory factors that make the process successful

How much to sample will depend on five major factors.

1. Method of sampling chosen
2. Desired confidence level
3. Desired precision of sampling
4. Time allocated to taking samples
5. Type of assessment desired (attribute vs. variable)

The depth and breadth of sample investigation depends on the scope of the audit.

How to Select an Unbiased Sample

Random selection permits each item in the population an equal chance of being selected and is, therefore, unbiased. A random sampling should be used after the process is running consistently. The random samples should be unbiased. When trying to establish what fast-food hamburger chain people like the best, an example of a biased sampling is asking people exiting a McDonald's restaurant as opposed to an unbiased sampling, which asks the same question via a telephone survey regarding all fast-food hamburger chains. There should be no preconditions on the selection of samples.

A random sample pulls a predetermined number of samples from the field. When performing an audit on documents, it may not be feasible to shuffle documents. An alternative is to shuffle numbers that correspond to the documents (population). The actual items can be picked using random number tables, a random number calculator, or by opening up the pages of a book and using those numbers to select random samples that correspond to the items under investigation.

Random number tables can be found in many sources such as Herbert Arkin's *Handbook of Sampling for Auditing and Accounting*. Appendix C is an excerpt from the *Table of 105,000 Random Decimal Digits* by Interstate Commerce Commission, of which 3500 random numbers are included.

Steps in Using the Random Number Tables in Appendix C

1. Establish the desired sample size.
2. Establish the range of sequential numbers of items to be investigated.

3. Based on the number of digits in the sequence numbers, the number of digits necessary to be used from the random number table will be contained in the largest number of that series.

4. Find a starting point in the table by opening the tables haphazardly and pointing your finger at any number on the page. This becomes the starting point.

5. By selecting numbers of sufficient digits, move either vertically down the column, horizontally across the row, or diagonally across the table until you have secured enough numbers to meet the sample size. As an example, if we wanted to investigate 50 invoice samples containing identification numbers between 278 and 5322, the number of digits we need is four, and we use the random number table as follows:

Starting arbitrarily at Row 1, Column 5, we use four digits of the number 01943, making the identification number of the first invoice used, 1943. We proceed down the column for the next sample identification number, which is 2153. Continuing down the column, the third number reads 9048. Since this number exceeds 5322, we disregard this as a valid sample number and move to the next number, which reads 3448. As this is a valid number for our use, it becomes the third sample identification number. Using this process, we continue moving down the column until 50 valid identification numbers are secured.

Endnotes

1. Arkin, *Handbook of Sampling*, 13–14.
2. Ibid., 89.
3. Ibid., 134.
4. Ibid., 140.

Epilogue

In closing, this book has provided the reader with a fundamental understanding of quality auditing concepts and techniques, TQM sample analysis, and SPC as it relates to the field of quality auditing. Since many people view auditing as something painful done to them by someone else, this book presents a positive view of quality auditing as a means of improving the quality system and enhancing continuous quality improvement efforts.

I hope that the use of this book will create a greater degree of uniformity in the practice and implementation of quality auditing, both internally and externally, and a greater appreciation for the uses of quality auditing.

Statistical and Analytical Process Control Formulas

STEPS IN CONSTRUCTION OF
CONTROL CHARTS AND CRITICAL FORMULAS

Variables Control Chart:

When samples are expressed in quantitative units of measurement, e.g., length, weight, time.

$\bar{X}$—R Chart =
Plotting the Average & Range of Data Collected

Calculate the Average ($\bar{X}$) and Range (R) of each subgroup:

$$\bar{X} = \frac{X_1 + X_2 + ... + X_n}{n} \qquad n = \# \text{ of samples}$$

$$R = X_{max} - X_{min}$$

Calculate the Average Range ($\bar{R}$) and the Process Average ($\bar{\bar{X}}$):

$$\bar{\bar{X}} = \frac{\bar{X}_1 + \bar{X}_2 + ... + \bar{X}_k}{k} \quad \begin{array}{l} k = \# \text{ of subgroups} \\ (20\text{–}25 \text{ groups}) \end{array}$$

$$\bar{R} = \frac{R_1 + R_2 + ... + R_k}{k}$$

Calculate the Control Limits:

$$UCL_{\bar{X}} = \bar{\bar{X}} + A_2\bar{R} \qquad LCL_{\bar{X}} = \bar{\bar{X}} - A_2\bar{R}$$
$$UCL_R = D_4\bar{R} \qquad\qquad LCL_R = D_3\bar{R}$$

Table of Factors for $\bar{X}$ & R Charts

Number of observations in subgroup (n)	Factors for X Chart	Factors for R Chart	
	A_2	Lower D_3	Upper D_4
2	1.880	0	3.268
3	1.023	0	2.574
4	0.729	0	2.282
5	0.577	0	2.114
6	0.483	0	2.004
7	0.419	0.076	1.924
8	0.373	0.136	1.864
9	0.337	0.184	1.816
10	0.308	0.223	1.777

Reprinted with permission from GOAL/QPC, 13 Branch Street, Methuen, MA 01844-1953. Source: *The Memory Jogger: A Pocket Guide of Tools for Continuous Improvement.* GOAL/QPC 1988.

STEPS IN CONSTRUCTION OF
CONTROL CHARTS AND CRITICAL FORMULAS

Attributes Control Chart:
When sample reflects **qualitative** characteristics, e.g., is/is not defective, go/no-go.

The *p* chart = proportion defective

$$p = \frac{\text{number of rejects in subgroups}}{\text{number inspected in subgroup}}$$

$$\bar{p} = \frac{\text{total number rejects}}{\text{total number inspected}}$$

$$UCL_p{}^* = \frac{\bar{p} + 3\sqrt{\bar{p}(1-\bar{p})}}{\sqrt{n}} \qquad LCL_p{}^* = \frac{\bar{p} - 3\sqrt{\bar{p}(1-\bar{p})}}{\sqrt{n}}$$

The *np* chart = number defective

$$UCL_{np} = n\bar{p} + 3\sqrt{n\bar{p}(1-\bar{p})} \qquad LCL_{np} = n\bar{p} - 3\sqrt{n\bar{p}(1-\bar{p})}$$

The *c* chart = Number nonconformities with a constant sample size

$$\bar{c} = \frac{\text{total nonconformities}}{\text{number of subgroups}}$$

$$UCL_c = \bar{c} + 3\sqrt{\bar{c}} \qquad LCL_c = \bar{c} - 3\sqrt{\bar{c}}$$

The *u* chart = Number nonconformities with varying sample size

$$\bar{u} = \frac{\text{total nonconformities}}{\text{total units inspected}}$$

$$UCL_u{}^* = \frac{\bar{u} + 3\sqrt{\bar{u}}}{\sqrt{n}} \qquad LCL_u{}^* = \frac{\bar{u} - 3\sqrt{\bar{u}}}{\sqrt{n}}$$

---

*This formula creates changing control limits. To avoid this, use Average Sample Sizes $\sqrt{n}$ for those samples that are ±20% of the average sample size. Calculate individual limits for the samples exceeding ±20%.

Reprinted with permission from GOAL/QPC, 13 Branch Street, Methuen, MA 01844-1953. Source: *The Memory Jogger: A Pocket Guide of Tools for Continuous Improvement.* GOAL/QPC 1988.

Quality Cost Analysis

From Jack Campanella, ed. *Principles of Quality Costs*, 2d ed. (Milwaukee, Wisc.: ASQC Quality Press. 1990), by permission of ASQC Quality Press.

Detailed Description of Quality Cost Elements

For future reference and use, detailed quality cost elements are identified in numerical sequence. Each element is not applicable to all businesses. It is up to the reader to determine applicability in each case. This list is not meant to contain every element of quality cost applicable to every business. It is intended to give the reader a general idea of the types of elements contained within each cost category to help decide individual classifications for actual use. If a significant cost exists that fits any part of the general description of the quality cost element, it should be used. In many cases, activities involve personnel from one or more departments. No attempt is made to define appropriate departments since each company is organized differently.

1.0 PREVENTION COSTS

The costs of all activities specifically designed to prevent poor quality in products or services.

1.1 *Marketing/Customer/User*

Costs incurred in the accumulation and continued evaluation of customer and user quality needs and perceptions (including feedback on reliability and performance) affecting their satisfaction with the company's product or service.

1.1.1 Marketing Research

The cost of that portion of marketing research devoted to the determination of customer and user quality needs—attributes of the product or service that provide a high degree of satisfaction.

1.1.2 Customer/User Perception Surveys/Clinics

The cost of programs designed to communicate with customers/ users for the expressed purpose of determining their perception of product or service quality as delivered and used, from the viewpoint of their expectations and needs relative to competitive offerings.

1.1.3 Contract/Document Review

Costs incurred in the review and evaluation of customer contracts or other documents affecting actual product or service requirements (such as applicable industry standards, government regulations, or customer internal specifications) to determine the company's capability to meet the stated requirements, prior to acceptance of the customer's terms.

1.2 *Product/Service/Design Development*

Costs incurred to translate customer and user needs into reliable quality standards and requirements and manage the quality of new product or service developments prior to the release of authorized documentation for initial production. These costs are normally planned and budgeted, and are applied to major design changes as well.

1.2.1 Design Quality Progress Reviews

The total cost, including planning, of interim and final design progress reviews, conducted to maximize conformance of product or service design to customer or user needs with regard to function, configuration, reliability, safety, producibility, unit cost, and, as applicable, serviceability, interchangeability, and maintainability. These formal reviews will occur prior to release of design documents for fabrication of prototype units or start of trial production.

1.2.2 Design Support Activities

The total cost of all activities specifically required to provide tangible quality support inputs to the product or service development effort. As applicable, design support activities include design document checking to ensure conformance to internal design standards; selection and design qualification of components and/or materials required as an integral part of the end-product or service; risk analyses for the safe use of end-product or service; producibility studies to ensure economic production capability; maintainability or serviceability analyses; reliability assurance activities such as failure mode and effects analysis and reliability apportionment; analysis of customer misuse and abuse potential; and preparation of an overall quality management plan.

1.2.3 Product Design Qualification Test

Costs incurred in the planning and conduct of the qualification testing of new products and major changes to existing products. Includes costs for the inspection and test of a sufficient quantity of qualification units under ambient conditions and the extremes of environmental parameters (worst-case conditions). Qualification inspections and tests are conducted to verify that all product design requirements have been met or, when failures occur, to clearly identify where redesign efforts are required. Qualification testing is performed on prototype units, pilot runs, or a sample of the initial production run of new products. (Some sources consider this an appraisal cost.)

1.2.4 Service Design—Qualification

Costs incurred in the qualification or overall process proving of new service offerings and major changes to existing offerings. Involves planning for and performing a pilot or trial run using prototype or first production supplies as required. Includes detailed measurements or observations of each aspect of the service offering under normal and worst-case conditions, for a sufficient quantity of units or time as applicable, to verify consistent conformance to requirements, or to identify where redesign efforts are required. (Some sources consider this an appraisal cost.)

1.2.5 Field Trials

The costs of planned observations and evaluation of end-product performance in trial situations—usually done with the cooperation of loyal customers but also includes sales into test markets. At this stage of product or service life, a company needs to know much more than: "Did it work?" or "Did it sell?" (Some sources consider this an appraisal cost.)

1.3 *Purchasing Prevention Costs*

Costs incurred to ensure conformance to requirements of supplier parts, materials, or processes, and to minimize the impact of supplier nonconformances on the quality of delivered products or services. Involves activities prior to and after finalization of purchase order commitments.

1.3.1 Supplier Reviews

The total cost of surveys to review and evaluate individual supplier's capabilities to meet company quality requirements. Usually conducted by a team of quality company representatives from affected departments. Can be conducted periodically for long-term associations.

1.3.2 Supplier Rating

The cost of developing and maintaining, as applicable, a system to ascertain each supplier's continued acceptability for future business. This rating system is based on actual supplier performance to established requirements, periodically analyzed, and given a quantitative or qualitative rating.

1.3.3 Purchase Order Tech Data Reviews

The cost for reviews of purchase order technical data (usually by other than purchasing personnel) to ensure its ability to clearly and completely communicate accurate technical and quality requirements to suppliers.

1.3.4 Supplier Quality Planning

The total cost of planning for the incoming and source inspections and tests necessary to determine acceptance of supplier products. Includes the preparation of necessary documents and development costs for newly required inspection and test equipment.

1.4 *Operations (Manufacturing or Service) Prevention Costs*

Costs incurred in ensuring the capability and readiness of operations to meet quality standards and requirements; quality control planning for all production activities; and the quality education of operating personnel.

1.4.1 Operations Process Validation

The cost of activities established for the purpose of ensuring the capability of new production methods, processes, equipment, machinery, and tools to initially and consistently perform within required limits.

1.4.2 Operations Quality Planning

The total cost for development of necessary product or service inspection, test, and audit procedures; appraisal documentation system; and workmanship or appearance standards to ensure the continued achievement of acceptable quality results. Also includes total design and development costs for new or special measurement and control techniques, gages, and equipment.

1.4.2.1 Design and Development of Quality Measurement and Control Equipment

The cost of test equipment engineers, planners, and designers; gage engineers; and inspection equipment engineers, planners, and designers.

1.4.3 Operations Support Quality Planning

The total cost of quality control planning for all activities required to provide tangible quality support to the production process. As applicable, these production support activities include, but are not limited to, preparation of specifications and the construction or purchase of new production equipment; preparation of operator instructions; scheduling and control plans for production supplies; laboratory analysis support; data processing support; and clerical support.

1.4.4 Operator Quality Education

Costs incurred in the development and conduct of formal operator training programs for the expressed purpose of preventing errors—programs that emphasize the value of quality and the role that each operator plays in its achievement. This includes operator training programs in subjects like statistical quality control, process control, quality circles, problem-solving techniques, etc. This item is not intended to include any portion of basic apprentice or skill training necessary to be qualified for an individual assignment within a company.

1.4.5 Operator SPC/Process Control

Costs incurred for education to implement program.

1.5 *Quality Administration*

Costs incurred in the overall administration of the quality management function.

1.5.1 Administrative Salaries

Compensation costs for all quality function personnel (such as managers, directors, supervisors, and clerical) whose duties are 100 percent administrative.

1.5.2 Administrative Expenses

All other costs and expenses charged to or allocated to the quality management function not specifically covered elsewhere in this system (such as heat, light, telephone).

1.5.3 Quality Program Planning

The cost of quality (procedure) manual development and maintenance, inputs to proposals, quality record keeping, strategic planning, and budget control.

1.5.4 Quality Performance Reporting

Costs incurred in quality performance data collection, compilation, analysis, and issuance in report forms designed to promote the continued improvement of quality performance. Quality cost reporting would be included in this category.

1.5.5 Quality Education

Costs incurred in the initial (new employee indoctrination) and continued quality education of all company functions that can affect the quality of product or service as delivered to customers. Quality education programs emphasize the value of quality performance and the role that each function plays in its achievement.

1.5.6 Quality Improvement

Costs incurred in the development and conduct of companywide quality improvement programs, designed to promote awareness of improvement opportunities and provide unique individual opportunities for participation and contributions.

1.5.7 Quality System Audits

The cost of audits performed to observe and evaluate the overall effectiveness of the quality management system and procedures. Often accomplished by a team of management personnel. Auditing of product is an appraisal cost. (See 2.2.1.)

1.6 *Other Prevention Costs*

Represents all other expenses of the quality system, not previously covered, specifically designed to prevent poor quality of product or service.

2.0 APPRAISAL COSTS

The costs associated with measuring, evaluating, or auditing products or services to ensure conformance to quality standards and performance requirements.

2.1 *Purchasing Appraisal Costs*

Purchasing appraisal costs generally can be considered as the costs incurred for the inspection and/or test of purchased supplies or services to determine acceptability for use. These activities can be performed as part of a receiving inspection function or as a source inspection at the supplier's facility.

2.1.1 Receiving or Incoming Inspections and Tests

Total costs for all normal or routing inspection and/or test of purchased materials, products, and services. These costs represent the baseline costs of purchased goods appraisal as a continuing part of a normal receiving inspection function.

2.1.2 Measurement Equipment

The cost of acquisition (depreciation or expense costs), calibration, and maintenance of measurement equipment, instruments, and gages used for appraisal of purchased supplies.

2.1.3 Qualification of Supplier Product

The cost of additional inspections or tests (including environmental tests) periodically required to qualify the use of production quantities of purchased goods. These costs are usually one-time costs but they may be repeated during multi-year production situations. The following are typical applications.

  a. First article inspection (detailed inspection and worst-case tests) on a sample of the first production buy of new components, materials, or services

  b. First article inspection for second and third sources of previously qualified and end-product key components

  c. First article inspection of the initial supply of customer-furnished parts or materials

  d. First article inspection of the initial purchased quantity of goods for resale

2.1.4 Source Inspection and Control Programs

All company-incurred costs (including travel) for the conduct of any of the activities described in 2.1.1 and 2.1.3 at the supplier's plant or at an independent test laboratory. This item will normally include all appraisal costs associated with direct shipments from supplier to the customer, sales office, or installation site.

2.2 *Operations (Manufacturing or Service) Appraisal Costs*

Operations appraisal costs generally can be considered as the costs incurred for the inspections, tests, or audits required to determine and ensure the acceptability of product or service to continue into each discrete step in the operations plan from start of production to delivery. In each case where material losses are an integral part of the appraisal operation, such as machine set-up pieces or destructive testing, the cost of the losses is to be included.

2.2.1 Planned Operations, Inspections, Tests, Audits

The cost of all planned inspections, tests, and audits conducted on product or service at selected points or work areas throughout the overall operations process including the point of final product or service acceptance. This is the baseline operations appraisal cost. It does not include the cost of troubleshooting, rework, repair, or sorting rejected lots, all of which are defined as failure costs.

2.2.1.1 Checking Labor

Work performed by individuals other than inspectors as in-process evaluation. Typically part of a production operator's job.

2.2.1.2 Product or Service Quality Audits

Personnel expense as a result of performing quality audits on inprocess or finished products or services.

2.2.1.3 Inspection and Test Materials

Materials consumed or destroyed in control of quality, e.g., by teardown inspections, over-voltage stressing, drop testing, or life testing.

2.2.2 Set-Up Inspections and Tests

The cost of all set-up or first piece inspections and tests utilized to ensure that each combination of machine and tool is properly adjusted to produce acceptable products before the start of each production lot, or that service processing equipment (including acceptance and test devices) is acceptable for the start of a new day, shift, or other time period.

2.2.3 Special Tests (Manufacturing)

The cost of all nonroutine inspections and tests conducted on manufactured product as a part of the appraisal plan. These costs normally include annual or semi-annual sampling of sensitive product for more detailed and extensive evaluations to ensure continued conformance to critical environmental requirements.

2.2.4 Process Control Measurements

The cost of all planned measurements conducted on in-line product or service processing equipment and/or materials (e.g., oven temperature or material density) to ensure conformance to preestablished standards. Includes adjustments made to maintain continued acceptable results.

2.2.5 Laboratory Support

The total cost of any laboratory tests required in support of product or service appraisal plans.

2.2.6 Measurement (Inspection and Test) Equipment

Since any measurement or process control equipment required is an integral part of appraisal operations, its acquisition (depreciation or expense), calibration, and maintenance costs are all included. Control of this equipment ensures the integrity of results, without which the effectiveness of the appraisal program would be in jeopardy.

2.2.6.1 Depreciation Allowances
Total depreciation allowances for all capitalized appraisal equipment.

2.2.6.2 Measurement Equipment Expenses
The procurement or build cost of all appraisal equipment and gages that are not capitalized.

2.2.6.3 Maintenance and Calibration Labor
The cost of all inspections, calibration, maintenance, and control of appraisal equipment, instruments, and gages used for the evaluation of support processes, products, or services for conformance to requirements.

2.2.7 Outside Endorsements and Certifications
The total cost of required outside endorsements or certifications, such as Underwriter's Laboratory, ASTM, or an agency of the US government. Includes the cost of sample preparation, submittal, and any liaison necessary to its final achievement. Includes cost of liaison with customers.

2.3 *External Appraisal Costs*
External appraisal costs will be incurred any time there is need for field setup or installation and checkout prior to official acceptance by the customer. These costs are also incurred when there is need for field trials of new products or services.

2.3.1 Field Performance Evaluation
The total cost of all appraisal efforts (inspections, tests, audits, and appraisal support activities) planned and conducted at the site for installation and/or delivery of large, complex products or the conduct of merchandised services (such as repairs or leasing set-ups).

2.3.2 Special Product Evaluations
Includes life testing, and environmental and reliability tests performed on production units.

2.3.3 Evaluation of Field Stock and Spare Parts
Includes cost of evaluation testing or inspection of field stock, resulting from engineering changes, storage time (excessive shelf life), or other suspected problems.

2.4 *Review of Test and Inspection Data*

Costs incurred for regularly reviewing inspection and test data prior to release of the product for shipment, such as determining whether product requirements have been met.

2.5 *Miscellaneous Quality Evaluations*

The cost of all support area quality evaluations (audits) to ensure continued ability to supply acceptable support to the production process. Examples of areas included are stores, packaging, and shipping.

3.0 INTERNAL FAILURE COSTS

Costs resulting from products or services not conforming to requirements or customer/user needs. Internal failure costs occur prior to delivery or shipment of the product, or the furnishing of a service, to the customer.

3.1 *Product/Service Design Failure Costs (Internal)*

Design failure costs can generally be considered as the unplanned costs that are incurred because of inherent design inadequacies in released documentation for production operations. They do not include billable costs associated with customer-directed changes (product improvements) or major redesign efforts (product upgrading) that are part of a company-sponsored marketing plan.

3.1.1 Design Corrective Action

After initial release of design for production, the total cost of all problem investigation and redesign efforts (including requalification as necessary) required to completely resolve product or service problems inherent in the design. (Some sources consider this a prevention cost.)

3.1.2 Rework Due to Design Changes

The cost of all rework (materials, labor, and applicable burden) specifically required as part of design problem resolutions and implementation plan (effectivity) for required design changes.

3.1.3 Scrap Due to Design Changes

The cost of all scrap (materials, labor, and applicable burden) required as part of design problem resolutions and implementation plan (effectivity) for design changes.

3.1.4 Production Liaison Costs

The cost of unplanned production support efforts required because of inadequate or incomplete design description and documentation by the design organization.

3.2 *Purchasing Failure Costs*

Costs incurred due to purchased item rejects.

3.2.1 Purchased Material Reject Disposition Costs

The cost to dispose of or sort incoming inspection rejects. Includes the cost of reject documentation, review and evaluation, disposition orders, handling, and transportation and expediting costs (when not paid for by the supplier).

3.2.2 Purchased Material Replacement Costs

The added cost of replacement for all items rejected and returned to supplier. Includes additional transportation and expediting costs (when not paid for by the supplier).

3.2.3 Supplier Corrective Action

The cost of company-sponsored failure analyses and investigations into the cause of supplier rejects to determine necessary corrective actions. Includes the cost of visits to supplier plants for this purpose and the cost to provide necessary added inspection protection while the problem is being resolved. (Some sources consider this a prevention cost.)

3.2.4 Rework of Supplier Rejects

The total cost of necessary supplier item repairs incurred by the company and not billable to the supplier—usually due to production expediencies.

3.2.5 Uncontrolled Material Losses

The cost of material or parts shortages due to damage, theft, or other (unknown) reasons. A measure of these costs may be obtained from reviews of inventory adjustments.

3.3 *Operations (Product or Service) Failure Costs*

Operations failure costs almost always represent a significant portion of overall quality costs and can generally be viewed as the costs associated with defective product or service discovered during the operations process. They are categorized into three distinct areas: material review and corrective action, rework/repair costs, and scrap costs.

3.3.1 Material Review and Corrective Action Costs

Costs incurred in the review and disposition of nonconforming product or service and the corrective actions necessary to prevent recurrence.

3.3.1.1 Disposition Costs

All costs incurred in the review and disposition of nonconforming product or service, in the analysis of quality data to determine significant areas for corrective action, and in the investigation of these areas to determine the root causes of the defective product or service.

3.3.1.2 Troubleshooting or Failure Analysis Costs (Operations)

The cost of failure analysis (physical, chemical, etc.) conducted by, or obtained from, outside laboratories in support of defect cause identification. (Some sources consider this a prevention cost.)

3.3.1.3 Investigation Support Costs

The additional cost of special runs of product or controlled lots of material (designed experiments) conducted specifically to obtain information useful to the determination of the root cause of a particular problem. (Some sources consider this a prevention cost.)

3.3.1.4 Operations Corrective Action

The actual cost of corrective actions taken to remove or eliminate the root causes of nonconformances identified for correction. This item can include such activities as rewriting operator instructions, redevelopment of specific processes or flow procedures, redesign or modification of equipment or tooling, and the development and implementation of specific training needs. Does not include design (3.1.1) or supplier (3.2.3) corrective action costs. (Some sources consider this a prevention costs.)

3.3.2 Operations Rework and Repair Costs

The total cost (labor, material, and overhead) of reworking or repairing defective product or service discovered within the operations process.

3.3.2.1 Rework

The total cost (material, labor, and burden) of all work done to bring nonconforming product or service up to an acceptable (conforming) condition, as authorized by specific work order, blueprint, personal assignment, or a planned part of the standard operating process. Does not include rework due to design change (3.1.2).

3.3.2.2 Repair

The total cost (material, labor, and burden) of all work done to bring nonconforming product up to an acceptable or equivalent, but still nonconforming, condition; normally accomplished by subjecting the product to an approved process that will reduce but not completely eliminate the nonconformance.

3.3.3 Reinspection/Retest Costs

That portion of inspection, test, and audit labor that is incurred because of rejects (includes documentation of rejects, reinspection or test after rework/repair, and sorting of defective lots).

3.3.4 Extra Operations

The total cost of extra operations, such as touch-up or trimming, added because the basic operation is not able to achieve conformance to requirements. These costs are often hidden in the accepted (standard) cost of operations.

3.3.5 Operations Scrap Costs

The total cost (material, labor; and overhead) of defective product or service that is wasted or disposed of because it cannot be reworked to conform to requirements. The unavoidable losses of material (such as the turnings from machining work or the residue in a food mixing pot) are generally known as waste (check company cost accounting definitions) and are not to be included in the cost of quality. Also, in the definition of quality costs, the amount received from the sale of scrap and waste material (salvage value) is not to be deducted from gross scrap failure costs.

3.3.6 Downgraded End-Product or Service

Price differential between normal selling price and reduced selling price due to nonconforming or off-grade end-products or services because of quality reasons. Also includes any costs incurred to bring up to saleable condition.

3.3.7 Internal Failure Labor Losses

When labor is lost because of nonconforming work, there may be no concurrent material losses and it is not reflected on scrap or rework reports. Accounting for the cost of labor for such losses is the intent of this item. Typical losses occur because of equipment shutdowns and reset-up or line stoppages for quality reasons and may be efficiency losses or even allocated for by "labor allowances."

3.4 *Other Internal Failure Costs*

4.0 EXTERNAL FAILURE COSTS

Costs resulting from products or services not conforming to requirements or customer/user needs. External failure costs occur after delivery or shipment of the product, and during or after furnishing of a service, to the customer.

4.1 *Complaint Investigations/Customer or User Service*

The total cost of investigating, resolving, and responding to individual customer or user complaints or inquiries, including necessary field service.

4.2 *Returned Goods*

The total cost of evaluating and repairing or replacing goods not meeting acceptance by the customer or user due to quality problems. It does not include repairs accomplished as part of a maintenance or modification contract.

4.3 *Retrofit Costs*

Costs to modify or update products or field service facilities to a new design change level, based on major redesign due to design deficiencies. Includes only that portion of retrofits that are due to quality problems.

4.3.1 Recall Costs

Includes costs of recall activity due to quality problems.

4.4 *Warranty Claims*

The total cost of claims paid to the customer or user, after acceptance, to cover expenses, including repair costs such as removing defective hardware from a system or cleaning costs due to a food or chemical service accident. In cases where a price reduction is negotiated in lieu of warranty, the value of this reduction should be counted.

4.5 *Liability Costs*

Company-paid costs due to liability claims, including the cost of product of service liability insurance.

4.6 *Penalties*

Cost of any penalties incurred because of less than full product or service performance achieved (as required by contracts with customers, or government rules and regulations).

4.7 *Customer/User Goodwill*

Costs incurred, over and above normal selling costs, to customers or users who are not completely satisfied with the quality of delivered product or service such as costs incurred because customers' quality expectations are greater than what they receive.

4.8 *Lost Sales*

Includes value of contribution margin lost due to sales reduction because of quality problems.

4.9 *Other External Failure Costs*

Detailed Quality Cost Element Summary

Prevention Costs

1.0	**Prevention Costs**
1.1	Marketing/Customer/User
1.1.1	Marketing Research
1.1.2	Customer/User Perception Surveys/Clinics
1.1.3	Contract/Document Review
1.2	Product/Service/Design Development
1.2.1	Design Quality Progress Reviews
1.2.2	Design Support Activities
1.2.3	Product Design Qualification Test
1.2.4	Service Design—Qualification
1.2.5	Field Trials
1.3	Purchasing Prevention Costs
1.3.1	Supplier Reviews
1.3.2	Supplier Rating
1.3.3	Purchase Order Tech Data Reviews
1.3.4	Supplier Quality Planning
1.4	Operations (Manufacturing or Service) Prevention Costs
1.4.1	Operations Process Validation
1.4.2	Operations Quality Planning
1.4.2.1	Design and Development of Quality Measurement and Control Equipment
1.4.3	Operations Support Quality Planning
1.4.4	Operator Quality Education
1.4.5	Operator SPC/Process Control
1.5	Quality Administration
1.5.1	Administrative Salaries
1.5.2	Administrative Expenses
1.5.3	Quality Program Planning
1.5.4	Quality Performance Reporting
1.5.5	Quality Education
1.5.6	Quality Improvement
1.5.7	Quality System Audits
1.6	Other Prevention Costs

Appraisal Costs

2.0	**Appraisal Costs**
2.1	Purchasing Appraisal Costs
2.1.1	Receiving or Incoming Inspections and Tests
2.1.2	Measurement Equipment
2.1.3	Qualification of Supplier Product
2.1.4	Source Inspection and Control Programs
2.2	Operations (Manufacturing or Service) Appraisal Costs
2.2.1	Planned Operations, Inspections, Tests, Audits
2.2.1.1	Checking Labor
2.2.1.2	Product or Service Quality Audits
2.2.1.3	Inspection and Test Materials
2.2.2	Set-Up Inspections and Tests
2.2.3	Special Tests (Manufacturing)
2.2.4	Process Control Measurements
2.2.5	Laboratory Support
2.2.6	Measurement (Inspection and Test) Equipment
2.2.6.1	Depreciation Allowances
2.2.6.2	Measurement Equipment Expenses
2.2.6.3	Maintenance and Calibration Labor
2.2.7	Outside Endorsements and Certifications
2.3	External Appraisal Costs
2.3.1	Field Performance Evaluation
2.3.2	Special Product Evaluations
2.3.3	Evaluation of Field Stock and Spare Parts
2.4	Review of Test and Inspection Data
2.5	Miscellaneous Quality Evaluations

Detailed quality cost element summary.

3.0	**Internal Failure Costs**
3.1	Product/Service Design Failure Costs (Internal)
3.1.1	Design Corrective Action
3.1.2	Rework Due to Design Changes
3.1.3	Scrap Due to Design Changes
3.1.4	Production Liaison Costs
3.2	Purchasing Failure Costs
3.2.1	Purchased Material Reject Disposition Costs
3.2.2	Purchased Material Replacement Costs
3.2.3	Supplier Corrective Action
3.2.4	Rework of Supplier Rejects
3.2.5	Uncontrolled Material Losses
3.3	Operations (Product or Service) Failure Costs
3.3.1	Material Review and Corrective Action Costs
3.3.1.1	Disposition Costs
3.3.1.2	Troubleshooting or Failure Analysis Costs (Operations)
3.3.1.3	Investigation Support Costs
3.3.1.4	Operations Corrective Action
3.3.2	Operations Rework and Repair Costs
3.3.2.1	Rework
3.3.2.2	Repair
3.3.3	Reinspection/Retest Costs
3.3.4	Extra Operations
3.3.5	Operations Scrap Costs
3.3.6	Downgraded End-Product or Service
3.3.7	Internal Failure Labor Losses
3.4	Other Internal Failure Costs

4.0	**External Failure Costs**
4.1	Complaint Investigations/Customer or User Service
4.2	Returned Goods
4.3	Retrofit Costs
4.3.1	Recall Costs
4.4	Warranty Claims
4.5	Liability Costs
4.6	Penalties
4.7	Customer/User Goodwill
4.8	Lost Sales
4.9	Other External Failure Costs

Detailed quality cost element summary (continued).

Random Number Tables

The following pages contain 3500 of 105,000 random numbers reproduced by the Interstate Commerce Commission with permission by the author and publisher, RAND Corporation, A Million Random Digits with 100,000 Normal Deviates, Glencoe Free Press Division of the Macmillan Company, New York, 1955.

Reprinted from the Interstate Commerce Commission, Bureau of Transportation, Economics, and Statistics, Washington, D.C. Public domain.

ROW	COL. (1)	(2)	(3)	(4)	(5)	(6)	(7)	(8)	(9)	(10)	(11)	(12)	(13)	(14)
1	34400	46986	53711	57781	01943	77050	23457	98083	98953	71788	14205	83463	02186	61093
2	47908	65561	83415	01504	72153	59572	99819	77525	32809	81582	64602	33916	11340	14275
3	86464	48476	31772	86087	59048	04163	38782	62570	05856	95629	19002	31835	75105	92491
4	88473	30746	25656	85895	83448	86869	37178	79378	84653	23701	80880	28839	53394	65672
5	84578	94139	02526	60885	45229	07655	82445	50670	94660	59042	67669	31500	29791	89193
6	47674	46019	77283	36578	94342	83834	75574	26193	59911	50710	42321	50204	06108	24417
7	35246	27327	43296	60039	94425	52613	71713	34601	77222	69706	91307	28008	01224	19341
8	68816	42794	53326	29909	80176	71268	82640	40943	55521	94982	03049	67227	31894	84383
9	66265	04312	76638	94348	29920	23832	76483	93438	31895	60649	83765	08752	34685	70680
10	04274	92021	41846	58537	18322	17797	73051	39905	99920	24216	92097	12727	16726	58214
11	40650	03900	19879	68313	05394	58565	12283	92471	48800	74252	84483	37631	69207	98166
12	94660	80071	38286	05872	29328	41573	95478	65178	72845	32647	83311	03398	89507	16672
13	66188	26224	36944	14097	03398	46855	97354	60641	67606	11670	11295	53619	69804	52287
14	28890	32302	16820	62604	88182	92710	85725	87612	62971	16558	16616	00708	11801	43421
15	19856	37877	62143	26406	32882	95658	66844	06072	48097	60632	31880	19330	88706	87627
16	59190	14722	56308	19063	30690	96710	83507	93018	70150	31555	49072	76270	46665	68317
17	16749	52782	22469	63127	47394	27855	41536	20409	96891	10913	75728	62763	05816	26918
18	49259	49778	31814	78246	74786	52723	98917	26733	25006	42075	06077	66781	25166	89663
19	45616	18113	96645	41768	28864	01172	11579	30164	60978	02497	79420	22510	83295	43047
20	01410	72952	29630	19950	40709	36754	10600	99734	54642	65177	60513	05667	18286	81571
21	70354	29470	84722	93751	22785	30285	65824	00125	31665	30783	32468	63251	22098	04434
22	63844	34598	59331	41928	30507	90271	83156	65363	32432	91628	71834	11228	36055	14594
23	75212	00957	56233	86984	96525	61563	24613	19613	34934	39500	60285	60193	90357	20507
24	22318	88151	61599	80848	85531	79779	96539	10170	01848	07056	21807	15934	95515	50838
25	52232	67825	10252	71921	42336	28144	77740	00526	71495	48308	22585	66481	44363	81179
26	87829	48053	72049	02527	65639	67289	73216	89299	64235	44811	51693	92645	60321	50674
27	73717	00239	31299	06934	39247	44953	81282	43648	47112	68961	95342	94312	43364	75848
28	06105	73489	19102	56385	09779	39198	68837	99016	22755	75257	58553	71429	89092	17044
29	40224	87176	25910	47068	90713	19370	02160	30265	83551	36320	46650	37654	95373	41488
30	82490	97718	29634	06600	60280	34991	30694	83119	08082	61327	74902	54735	98259	15092
31	76559	35273	51185	56238	61135	40181	02053	35637	30071	16931	63393	55452	60508	45962
32	68971	99161	69525	09420	95761	80565	93073	02443	80398	66799	05705	46922	18300	59981
33	82616	17495	44660	94322	31862	26318	20115	59225	62709	43548	46112	60905	94684	52444
34	71487	09441	11059	87092	47405	89244	98072	33419	56339	43045	71639	42422	23714	94883
35	95214	46497	99594	99508	01324	20627	73975	98818	48110	25701	47204	38896	22197	21015
36	59629	83335	06139	47008	94316	65703	06028	89416	90721	90664	86650	97178	57317	00664
37	66350	87472	00603	62030	80251	07857	09806	96366	09060	70760	64614	99659	35525	99770
38	26286	02763	15423	38413	94858	49874	39754	02355	12203	09829	53494	38703	58607	38568
39	54666	11022	17445	95352	05883	78057	26919	91872	33285	29723	05900	12042	63733	82699
40	64588	25333	86007	49143	22433	00740	38629	35541	26899	92681	63599	04319	49091	04166
41	05837	98076	10308	51393	22322	63421	47196	40458	08474	68660	33098	43742	34064	08665
42	90206	33368	52172	49146	47800	99830	65932	77581	42783	64140	51143	89799	62899	61267
43	15943	46255	68072	39374	60860	42702	35689	66370	50839	18343	50860	91106	13819	97061
44	43408	84725	26739	90782	06671	68971	97540	51875	86377	13414	28515	65096	61292	60307
45	86614	31253	52059	67938	50891	03215	42456	52218	06491	56614	15390	43427	59804	82456
46	24314	98658	55919	68944	72508	12783	83486	16386	96663	96064	00285	47240	83375	20432
47	48405	30581	45615	82627	55035	32483	99222	06146	20348	83834	09024	41148	72267	52551
48	04681	40804	63227	82560	37831	00009	95326	22887	81584	93916	36514	23804	23542	77777
49	57770	30655	92344	50017	67171	33804	97346	10885	95755	54498	99474	91670	16465	25454
50	97203	06653	94961	29477	26517	87514	20248	64475	89899	79724	86043	59012	71297	68910

ROW	COL.	(1)	(2)	(3)	(4)	(5)	(6)	(7)	(8)	(9)	(10)	(11)	(12)	(13)	(14)
51		51645	98661	88422	26248	45198	97112	45964	90089	33098	97772	40550	53760	85879	20708
52		74535	68977	91426	42636	37570	46742	24752	95509	91849	57785	95421	88518	29311	11910
53		82073	36081	48877	06766	41307	17197	61531	53971	59280	42311	63183	66223	19937	66014
54		26780	26262	06010	86755	02820	27335	73665	49199	06690	99820	56432	62150	56003	61085
55		24380	65621	11298	07821	32725	54464	15733	72871	40300	23936	84752	94750	55405	21262
56		25691	31722	21715	01059	30389	64211	85558	24496	71369	97464	75959	66324	72381	43577
57		22564	64528	96588	75722	41460	88123	53507	93663	56136	99007	92388	60971	68037	35312
58		83497	98701	96442	60874	82103	41350	52770	50953	57656	94747	74469	91798	65091	22432
59		77841	37239	28922	77915	50378	54787	17897	04064	97463	68605	39642	31647	82528	75480
60		08456	44896	96370	01327	66730	74615	51954	21716	45985	15824	72338	98537	51112	71728
61		47770	38347	32186	08630	45220	36517	95131	83329	59349	76898	80836	30521	56718	81620
62		18352	95404	86417	06379	62319	21663	13592	56974	87497	53620	26778	6400	90764	38105
63		13716	62729	33795	87160	98516	76882	49223	25004	88223	64613	32985	26814	51833	57363
64		86675	38742	39639	67704	03454	22996	92696	35795	77185	45750	60438	60026	72498	71331
65		75188	55511	94496	01498	15935	45228	62286	91563	35899	92588	74107	65389	41614	16567
66		55904	45492	93459	97948	26999	63484	22844	26405	51929	89432	51722	49793	75248	49617
67		22701	43144	30281	94746	55393	51025	39757	51729	68780	71962	10119	94807	23987	99253
68		12717	94106	62367	71530	94688	68341	00996	64154	21125	04256	28516	45108	31054	51464
69		49961	51838	48316	20781	28576	18868	61128	74465	50206	60516	74018	61495	56744	30314
70		48999	29283	83865	22337	07139	95196	82131	13811	40242	20798	84394	31145	33299	87324
71		55961	82953	20233	04375	17186	25370	16016	35583	85838	95160	29268	16720	23491	51865
72		21933	05232	26712	60326	57323	80074	90224	90626	41720	95492	00915	94184	13522	05444
73		97588	19936	36998	70085	03359	01499	78540	72507	66917	93777	06973	40149	88415	46652
74		65625	02979	39658	91885	09402	09437	01902	17090	42654	12374	34131	41948	93503	47153
75		54964	21944	73133	59918	89088	02230	69171	77290	91446	70513	27072	25129	57959	45194
76		40108	38874	51549	33380	36759	74101	19766	41145	11203	10552	20711	60184	42047	61072
77		62990	13609	14721	12927	89204	74279	25363	11559	29631	86798	60793	44009	05015	50160
78		33452	45811	07170	60596	20041	45099	52672	33458	92808	84166	61385	80712	94125	92235
79		45269	97040	90933	96731	87447	27430	65569	02641	96505	58735	13951	26022	31272	70780
80		58495	29888	59912	42917	15655	07771	54955	92720	46600	87194	66025	43420	99342	75754
81		78134	56125	43499	32638	08171	85049	66694	76578	31646	61340	74238	00516	53544	98535
82		72714	09574	08735	34154	74287	54923	14709	53315	38631	77190	89442	78117	34602	76921
83		58725	52894	58855	65454	27725	77914	67632	09279	86769	97446	86697	68616	57404	82700
84		04920	90562	67101	44369	22056	38938	01568	98190	72194	30497	43306	60737	27021	51197
85		93281	62076	34032	44247	99897	59109	18307	43087	41275	30140	24410	24436	71556	97860
86		24559	61198	66069	32886	05127	74741	04046	48701	27859	09807	60598	50584	21094	01321
87		78630	00100	40308	52577	04223	94567	36894	64381	36040	04751	63577	34160	52345	52003
88		59891	80115	62671	56700	10840	70508	00551	91190	95870	56924	83977	82451	49249	05270
89		54493	68947	86624	67430	23663	45753	36595	82839	83724	56702	42278	13147	11025	57913
90		75617	34112	64745	30812	08118	58561	75445	23039	33555	14437	52574	05475	62920	09254
91		56106	60085	92164	34083	29202	55683	54393	09647	53667	27932	07273	94264	84217	08005
92		01573	83192	96421	82875	27850	35990	71408	20683	33995	62717	14966	24940	78231	13101
93		43088	59995	39776	18120	61214	34708	39593	90146	09006	28201	04526	79146	14721	57421
94		25962	59796	23122	36236	06817	73889	25531	97865	40911	77093	79405	02329	71405	93773
95		88709	82726	83052	16697	76219	29988	08235	12756	26073	11957	57101	06000	83645	51908
96		49788	84563	09560	39128	03807	93571	00206	50823	24135	30841	35844	59568	22233	32425
97		45352	17163	73899	60419	91377	72508	96361	46184	09305	62505	18408	09234	34770	40516
98		13593	56221	93394	21842	88707	13474	17645	96492	54038	38312	01771	02093	89548	01052
99		40241	32180	85013	59035	74849	19454	69521	78460	58521	79904	75369	37522	30959	60932
100		99416	36186	38334	40023	57769	98729	32765	53902	59679	63698	18970	27192	66875	87303

ROW	COL.	(1)	(2)	(3)	(4)	(5)	(6)	(7)	(8)	(9)	(10)	(11)	(12)	(13)	(14)
101		99576	03093	87527	35848	71876	21027	42002	67787	17981	67468	87429	81377	22996	43586
102		69704	95249	20426	55681	48290	56229	51269	93367	13304	62412	58287	91145	74044	73706
103		44543	06981	64923	94700	18579	34495	92207	46201	83687	45565	51345	82679	85959	58707
104		60805	54760	49291	35370	31358	53728	48837	22398	78577	34699	94709	77225	49119	59636
105		40692	55578	31932	31631	99065	59480	11434	94820	33320	48576	85772	87197	77476	86304
106		64109	17486	07580	90241	25288	67441	63958	26040	72928	58371	44130	68856	84927	08921
107		47570	64977	11839	81049	14859	45800	93519	56783	26678	95403	71505	97496	44242	62072
108		33130	39631	56393	41573	90914	28526	40997	43082	84646	00789	64943	12781	40642	46583
109		11636	25414	07362	35505	53651	23549	59229	02636	94269	67293	10140	13163	92380	98525
110		86815	46792	68828	32135	09493	95685	40409	47342	21559	81035	02601	84804	30947	70588
111		84167	05822	78593	71579	71522	17517	34760	26696	68553	63587	71741	48249	03605	81257
112		20901	53017	63203	17806	46713	33609	28888	39065	45852	41570	15574	07082	19542	60725
113		49319	56431	40655	18391	61770	46077	35487	25332	03194	16694	72195	68767	60846	08353
114		44052	49228	15868	07676	14994	39430	71803	79499	34989	51312	43646	55384	76359	07399
115		78899	85420	93118	33521	11608	50190	09894	77582	90196	22745	50201	89343	95604	32522
116		53664	24220	82877	11621	35505	32810	59665	42479	75120	42638	21884	09397	95109	51780
117		60576	79805	24509	92685	75800	57765	08333	81168	50606	36877	27642	32199	80919	80059
118		40917	46217	04820	20523	24956	43686	40304	01939	26727	90083	89658	80329	02180	54181
119		83426	65760	00098	29270	54332	33983	08605	52378	97373	23578	01837	82029	98140	60385
120		00997	61617	06272	00283	67396	91682	15334	73062	04327	58763	22529	54432	50704	00393
121		05078	55974	42408	34593	59319	84423	15322	92885	53548	71959	89729	54175	98683	72919
122		15565	90647	55917	05217	11039	86111	26083	49670	60226	09534	25500	60560	61431	52963
123		17339	53708	34099	75573	86717	02524	19945	79265	02488	79953	80302	89644	46540	16807
124		56452	13100	23947	31330	97352	12165	01178	98728	13430	64012	35392	18601	48424	38352
125		52728	68665	57473	88285	23203	22955	22663	49092	42908	33008	57726	68825	61025	59688
126		82248	97726	61171	43512	87690	90678	35602	23875	99422	11651	13820	15146	53615	53669
127		08901	58755	10916	45305	58545	18433	47966	08760	01278	87437	46856	55444	71266	62145
128		30298	39266	92759	37734	00120	61037	86899	17415	06817	18632	61681	48935	80782	90394
129		81530	13448	84528	88326	01377	97714	28500	97816	90649	78734	04677	11133	53531	55173
130		79066	67657	09236	33158	96525	14018	80175	31636	61015	86412	39718	63445	35994	68769
131		14279	24885	58579	17943	07595	51012	20380	63247	12178	31085	80369	34225	63824	45202
132		71864	22790	83751	30368	54572	74015	29667	41559	87682	28442	87856	81308	43384	29251
133		18646	64041	00409	14055	03256	47490	95518	34369	89408	26508	99385	31516	08535	60250
134		95778	60721	65813	87273	20365	83095	13697	04304	66848	17562	44031	21737	53724	15510
135		48007	18612	35935	11227	39374	12775	28208	21336	32669	80081	50999	47643	40494	28572
136		21737	45755	06128	83436	40132	01427	06347	17155	68153	03777	17467	85951	60096	02395
137		87771	10353	64235	16128	50645	50222	18978	81714	78932	78062	38822	81509	70976	75452
138		69755	18943	14511	48794	86155	29481	56795	46026	12540	40574	33676	63008	01494	72848
139		06497	22983	27966	22367	18364	12653	54729	05231	05388	44111	66004	29182	44290	42727
140		96697	40071	08001	41981	03252	71621	62136	34493	20664	65314	72806	24344	96307	44584
141		36304	06446	40997	47621	51865	71890	29982	69908	04060	38463	74700	24059	50789	17342
142		90223	19769	54918	90841	67059	99721	23197	64944	55434	33794	06032	81736	72132	46101
143		86698	04288	26064	40488	25475	27360	72277	81634	36203	33117	06823	06544	13879	15911
144		87522	76756	43040	03352	84467	03667	87826	02443	82917	04893	71743	31948	41667	72370
145		41834	02156	59983	77733	07388	63549	92520	75717	60182	14970	53483	43361	01102	92482
146		84047	00169	19880	84733	84577	80659	40150	25786	05056	71017	13763	36051	46982	32627
147		08804	86781	21383	30659	58566	19380	25687	20464	36204	32625	19783	63388	50327	78278
148		27463	95419	78419	19803	01643	33681	56628	83989	97143	61743	23935	81230	23400	63258
149		84239	12011	98138	07106	49747	75629	17739	01264	01451	16487	30560	29425	73541	20812
150		92657	18659	04162	26698	41464	30442	24556	88843	28193	19250	04273	85799	45735	96143

COL. ROW	(1)	(2)	(3)	(4)	(5)	(6)	(7)	(8)	(9)	(10)	(11)	(12)	(13)	(14)
151	63056	10872	34173	34711	97853	44519	04719	06062	52485	40668	65229	67388	13630	31285
152	05609	36515	95349	12459	75635	14825	37640	11132	61530	74353	12139	32768	14748	32643
153	18645	30934	03621	93974	07681	79546	20312	77671	84900	07433	48177	34799	56395	45904
154	81049	60454	53475	52989	05942	86098	01894	64991	73777	88048	59712	07386	38120	40400
155	88979	45354	09433	58219	58385	84393	15541	52487	80394	28432	98066	13352	15232	19515
156	07703	29701	74967	11838	69735	24841	49329	42244	44807	01227	34839	04940	94889	97039
157	00350	98959	62466	11908	44818	37797	38411	47706	24596	02459	51452	11977	82701	69490
158	85256	63805	86437	07118	28777	43846	74313	42405	85560	03695	91191	17812	81187	84009
159	22295	88219	57387	70375	66870	37373	48808	41364	81509	24729	27143	15833	09826	13466
160	89096	42312	67426	65525	51782	80824	89794	99668	04919	15674	97591	77524	24085	58054
161	39013	38665	83216	11383	09030	64072	53461	25606	56999	50117	58191	76295	44324	90840
162	72491	15352	00703	16138	56402	78573	79778	90916	95455	41713	92549	85983	41628	75816
163	23826	47354	07115	26274	45738	92800	76014	49663	24905	75827	50031	92503	14938	62377
164	46283	59514	88312	45799	88822	02950	26397	56784	48229	06134	54479	27989	44177	67192
165	36411	02093	55967	29373	70291	66217	81482	70084	76146	23839	78376	83643	99785	36650
166	35119	52279	32144	38485	37645	51525	14593	98897	02358	68254	67959	02954	29884	39249
167	80163	74919	32030	36445	78416	12325	43795	11467	38768	52200	29480	61690	14876	81480
168	59732	46850	41924	34384	22821	53260	50143	62797	79755	02039	03286	15187	27034	65416
169	36192	06134	58583	66187	33493	41852	10775	96679	75021	13830	40848	40848	91874	31098
170	89935	91342	25189	49290	82407	99826	79082	84087	21838	58295	82487	32206	65012	84098
171	89946	13976	26995	87999	72481	39971	05017	36061	56051	29158	86878	74287	61423	77863
172	04107	53615	54286	58385	16780	09442	03031	06632	23143	07798	42457	12186	67632	27661
173	97446	40662	30398	78240	33296	35025	74076	11792	13307	50383	51398	62265	21101	59545
174	54673	98461	67494	60763	98604	81780	42273	85806	98161	07963	47215	08274	86282	84259
175	08489	75101	00671	19712	61744	52401	24524	79664	11046	19760	45621	26852	33781	85917
176	31820	96220	03272	26581	78097	72107	55619	26792	06097	39837	29382	37929	17134	73696
177	31732	37369	51306	93270	05700	18907	21848	25477	93051	75333	66178	13305	16612	59642
178	68967	63104	55412	60291	33018	83050	34498	96186	07377	84214	79065	82451	71937	06951
179	37376	68508	99304	79353	81625	03672	11824	37381	26202	94938	95938	92934	35466	49965
180	55216	10408	27310	36026	51011	38992	31137	04099	90320	16690	48647	23436	57051	40620
181	28656	18962	67973	00480	15666	12512	92129	52487	96247	54405	28974	80959	35743	09827
182	21649	39352	02802	07741	48996	70996	29783	43060	70957	71339	27765	77007	37198	22386
183	85928	81409	47569	63650	70406	38158	99977	50397	81640	60534	47152	61161	55650	59326
184	93726	47599	89215	92599	89339	61017	00142	45481	84572	53086	32838	41376	73172	87202
185	70486	82498	92822	10969	03000	08607	97309	20070	47863	33083	79488	92605	66000	56618
186	09208	85060	26710	82939	95725	89481	47604	79244	05028	95766	16939	07170	29552	29011
187	05365	51267	26154	51796	48400	06773	50640	33933	44343	50720	21345	30048	90614	09192
188	85339	00049	36076	14481	07938	11842	32976	54614	51277	89792	69745	73460	20811	75371
189	94174	75628	64919	09046	80142	93381	60246	82213	16110	83203	16518	52348	64749	46778
190	12066	64440	24460	56820	90778	27159	50936	30047	37308	50265	91696	32931	77526	40245
191	71104	33982	95397	98007	39251	03285	41941	50700	52141	28468	06451	89499	97397	87452
192	56140	97304	69970	28698	33440	37466	34077	46788	14641	43632	76933	81226	15337	01676
193	17284	31319	86632	45843	50783	79384	11531	62407	10411	84253	37488	03628	43494	31862
194	77765	38319	58683	60125	13182	77783	15034	86720	80690	46932	83826	08549	97184	46069
195	74514	47141	04583	29966	61762	12470	81578	42151	05470	57768	23751	27586	77320	67981
196	87899	42644	62412	10724	67503	17035	26854	59971	37938	40472	21018	58106	41902	04214
197	32752	47903	88466	47118	67695	24737	70448	02898	12417	44840	15726	89205	29248	80865
198	32583	08623	04384	44980	30841	20804	90509	49558	77569	07387	63887	07348	56384	43152
199	79519	70114	44634	21886	21823	32813	88713	10771	32044	19104	59577	12182	41503	13629
200	35683	73286	28939	48003	10264	01551	84204	25717	52587	90723	64079	32263	78436	38479

COL. ROW	(1)	(2)	(3)	(4)	(5)	(6)	(7)	(8)	(9)	(10)	(11)	(12)	(13)	(14)
201	19822	87838	72597	48703	99122	03762	88425	46825	47125	58751	33421	56920	30427	52752
202	65546	31475	62734	77916	20639	67894	92147	05045	97056	32884	31868	67305	10171	24717
203	89963	35365	99047	58625	97134	81676	28030	27266	35993	21471	71367	36594	53508	58035
204	04777	47580	26132	92047	87918	18054	46676	17718	81388	97382	27633	76425	14941	63109
205	14366	92746	32577	65574	66778	47179	08192	03209	63913	12546	16285	55566	46560	30697
206	90777	73287	79780	90095	24465	67813	30140	02045	13234	06324	05404	12376	00846	28666
207	91479	51557	48230	58905	97790	80578	87702	20408	43401	60708	74147	25790	30271	99679
208	79371	79751	94621	35673	90372	94752	27865	43315	87138	40934	76588	43717	44528	19191
209	55323	84917	11433	76935	71895	68299	42471	74012	40611	55537	52638	78038	16448	61131
210	84906	09847	31539	45956	64239	81931	27254	20211	59279	45826	90804	21290	27172	84922
211	05236	64402	66160	52109	45415	81095	48946	27854	01235	67407	58721	09308	79589	04051
212	93093	43121	57400	54854	93240	97060	75142	99455	56650	19644	06058	43175	04645	42662
213	93486	60829	03157	69923	70047	13997	46941	45850	94221	85549	77513	61190	92464	31271
214	94152	71616	45272	58414	62161	80004	82963	28324	97351	59590	69590	55850	17392	52570
215	14657	11144	32580	44355	70403	30991	05430	43339	04991	78003	10598	26775	10921	11423
216	73802	18543	24002	16309	70512	39483	31704	12110	77598	88881	40277	37527	90999	29975
217	26532	55230	35064	46512	48635	75257	82965	89961	85315	27708	72514	21208	73954	05518
218	94748	23030	12740	69531	78549	68743	55640	51821	70438	96156	57729	05308	39347	13301
219	60650	22184	91742	33207	92010	46218	04053	85454	63852	18869	65565	19066	14169	47367
220	99059	33212	28131	94043	54163	59625	95437	65171	29377	64460	29935	81314	16326	32006
221	35486	55672	10532	84521	89120	29646	01152	49583	54988	47917	86745	04442	68931	26314
222	69343	22524	92528	76934	18068	47263	29952	04675	48205	92060	33419	27448	72842	57277
223	94815	62525	99667	17573	18334	43595	14368	55917	38915	94075	73443	36106	50357	14333
224	99200	92673	02042	42351	39262	24514	64590	63735	49055	84010	30249	66720	40387	69691
225	04206	71123	61509	54395	60738	20487	94087	53873	75837	01349	05592	25911	95667	89355
226	05059	07104	98080	75289	03790	88690	75218	35663	04940	00808	63264	89590	71383	65840
227	59277	38137	27494	92864	22086	24743	50733	73540	33611	68064	44706	46514	79035	27126
228	99276	27754	77135	01042	32302	86207	65802	57361	00412	98380	81887	26588	70230	45346
229	15968	70254	77877	61475	78551	83814	43745	89998	22524	63071	28657	77493	25019	75280
230	37387	33553	25694	46721	05188	92921	37764	05458	83683	44571	68022	46927	97771	55404
231	00295	31023	76244	82409	80188	64541	01822	41799	10283	89285	24480	58265	23209	54663
232	37073	29678	82758	80902	00963	04830	93988	66534	68701	38047	55487	28369	61313	21615
233	65424	57801	40586	03546	51923	25572	12361	35231	13037	66040	17727	55659	68304	70472
234	97272	38347	49125	31865	19892	42208	95888	09376	09935	55536	68273	20688	08906	08845
235	30046	46869	63999	18168	36404	85929	20239	30835	65719	62321	97146	41292	71724	70360
236	35192	73039	23402	87921	61958	11470	46768	52253	50245	19139	03288	67631	08986	74427
237	50144	69238	80552	43965	90923	17348	77645	21748	60485	09236	47403	08548	16397	69514
238	68654	47181	34922	54600	35947	83288	15345	78581	24488	69511	83557	40297	89854	46509
239	71423	23618	62167	64730	26658	00600	90175	28997	09530	24834	17749	01891	90239	63086
240	87384	27226	75828	36494	08916	44307	75639	01491	59832	25021	11042	77069	98992	04690
241	63991	16671	39873	49926	30858	23037	55243	68169	65607	00462	73453	79679	50667	36695
242	74676	63670	00942	39510	74960	70072	17979	11410	56398	86081	16441	52139	20793	07286
243	00300	70583	23618	23433	80245	77008	34920	98732	77093	99112	82202	72094	78922	48471
244	48893	80583	58252	01393	31708	84000	43153	67084	46423	27272	02851	01952	35100	18463
245	82238	45847	87466	23512	58267	56070	36755	75675	24235	09113	60652	08225	64698	20609
246	68820	34391	85076	42094	88085	97117	27431	06364	73098	44126	40115	55362	51469	79857
247	90781	71865	58177	16697	81043	67389	08356	00446	82067	31550	34714	51450	90412	88368
248	45723	87694	89291	70943	81970	34659	90028	67625	54875	97581	52870	30346	47856	82322
249	91645	33833	27129	27581	09107	38200	28833	33781	14627	51856	22921	43055	40101	45633
250	34627	22965	51179	61197	89764	40687	23585	85834	65165	47921	82521	19089	49399	51001

Tables for Estimating Sample Size for Attribute (Estimation Sampling)

Source: Herbert Arkin, *Handbook of Sampling for Auditing and Accounting*, 3d ed. Englewood Cliffs, N.J.: Prentice Hall (a division of Simon & Schuster), 1984. Used with permission.

Table D.1a. Sample sizes for sampling attributes for random samples only. Expected rate of occurrence not over 2 percent or expected rate of occurrence not less than 98 percent. Confidence level 90 percent (two-sided).

Population size	Sample size for precision of					
	±.5%	±.75%	±1%	±1.25%	±1.5%	±2%
200					109	80
250					122	87
300				160	133	92
350				173	141	97
400				184	149	100
450				194	155	103
500			258	203	161	105
550			271	210	166	107
600			282	217	170	109
650			293	223	173	111
700			302	229	177	112
750			311	234	180	113
800			319	239	183	114
850			327	243	185	115
900		461	334	247	187	116
950		474	341	251	189	117
1,000		486	347	254	191	118
1,250		538	373	267	199	120
1,500		579	392	277	204	122
1,750		613	408	285	208	124
2,000		641	420	291	211	125
2,100	1,055	651	424	293	212	125
2,500	1,148	685	438	299	216	126
3,000	1,243	718	451	305	219	127
3,500	1,321	743	461	310	221	128
4,000	1,387	764	465	313	223	129
4,500	1,442	780	475	316	224	129
5,000	1,490	794	480	318	226	130
7,500	1,654	838	496	325	229	131
10,000	1,751	862	504	329	231	131
12,500	1,814	877	509	331	232	132
15,000	1,859	888	513	332	233	132
20,000	1,919	901	517	334	233	132
30,000	1,982	915	522	336	234	133
40,000	2,015	922	524	337	235	133
50,000	2,036	926	525	338	235	133
75,000	2,064	932	527	338	235	133
100,000	2,078	935	528	339	236	133
150,000	2,092	938	529	339	236	133
200,000	2,100	939	529	339	236	133
300,000	2,107	940	530	340	236	133
500,000	2,113	942	530	340	236	133

Table D.1b. Sample sizes for sampling attributes for random samples only. Expected rate of occurrence not over 5 percent or expected rate of occurrence not less than 95 percent. Confidence level 90 percent (two-sided).

Population size	Sample size for precision of						
	±.5%	±1%	±1.5%	±2%	±2.5%	±3%	±4%
150						74	53
200					102	84	58
250					113	91	61
300				156	123	97	64
350				168	130	102	66
400				179	136	106	67
450				188	142	109	69
500				196	146	112	70
550				203	150	114	71
600				210	154	116	71
650			305	216	157	118	72
700			315	221	160	119	73
750			325	225	162	120	73
800			334	230	164	122	74
850			342	234	166	123	74
900			350	237	168	124	74
950			357	241	170	125	75
1,000			364	244	171	125	75
1,100			377	249	172	127	75
1,200		621	388	254	176	128	76
1,500		693	414	265	181	131	77
1,700		732	428	271	184	132	77
2,000		783	445	277	187	134	78
2,500		849	466	285	191	136	78
2,900		891	478	290	193	137	79
3,500		941	492	295	195	138	79
4,050		976	501	298	196	138	79
4,700		1,010	510	301	198	139	79
5,000	2,535	1,023	513	302	198	139	80
6,000	2,769	1,059	522	306	199	140	80
7,500	3,051	1,098	531	309	201	141	80
10,000	3,396	1,139	541	312	202	141	80
13,000	3,685	1,170	548	314	203	142	80
15,000	3,830	1,184	551	315	203	142	80
20,000	4,091	1,208	556	317	204	142	81
30,000	4,390	1,233	561	318	205	143	81
40,000	4,556	1,246	564	319	205	143	81
50,000	4,663	1,254	565	320	205	143	81
100,000	4,891	1,270	569	321	206	143	81
200,000	5,013	1,278	570	321	206	143	81
300,000	5,055	1,280	571	321	206	143	81
500,000	5,090	1,283	571	322	206	143	81

Table D.1c. Sample sizes for sampling attributes for random samples only. Expected rate of occurrence not over 10 percent or expected rate of occurrence not less than 90 percent. Confidence level 90 percent (two-sided).

Population size	Sample size for precision of						
	±.5%	±1%	±1.5%	±2%	±2.5%	±3%	±4%
250							95
300						143	101
350						153	108
400					198	162	111
450					209	169	114
500					219	176	117
550					229	182	120
600					237	187	122
650					244	192	124
700				326	251	196	126
750				337	257	199	127
800				346	263	203	128
850				355	268	206	130
900				364	272	209	131
950				372	277	211	132
1,000				379	281	213	133
1,050				386	285	216	133
1,100			546	392	288	218	134
1,250			581	410	298	223	136
1,400			611	425	306	227	138
1,500			629	434	310	230	139
1,750			669	452	319	235	141
2,000			703	467	327	239	142
2,400			746	486	336	244	144
2,500		1234	756	490	337	245	144
2,700		1281	773	497	341	246	145
3,000		1345	796	507	345	249	145
3,500		1437	827	519	351	252	146
4,000		1514	852	529	356	254	147
5,000		1638	890	543	362	257	148
7,500		1839	946	564	371	262	150
9,500		1939	972	573	375	264	150
10,000	4935	1959	977	574	376	264	150
15,000	5907	2096	1010	586	380	266	151
20,000	6551	2172	1027	591	383	267	152
30,000	7354	2253	1045	597	385	269	152
40,000	7834	2296	1055	600	386	269	152
50,000	8154	2323	1060	602	387	270	152
100,000	8877	2378	1071	606	389	270	152
200,000	9290	2407	1077	608	389	271	153
350,000	9478	2419	1080	608	390	271	153
500,000	9556	2424	1081	609	390	271	153

Table D.1d. Sample sizes for sampling attributes for random samples only. Expected rate of occurrence not over 20 percent or expected rate of occurrence not less than 80 percent. Confidence level 90 percent (two-sided).

Population size	Sample size for precision of						
	±1%	±1.5%	±2%	±2.5%	±3%	±4%	±5%
200							92
250							103
300						143	110
350						153	116
400						162	121
450						169	126
500					245	176	129
550					257	182	132
600					267	187	135
650					278	192	137
700				349	286	196	139
750				358	294	199	141
800				372	301	203	143
850				382	308	206	144
900				392	314	209	146
950				401	320	211	147
1,000				410	325	213	148
1,050				418	330	216	149
1,100			546	426	335	218	150
1,250			581	446	348	223	153
1,500			629	474	365	230	156
1,750			669	497	378	235	158
1,900			690	508	384	237	159
1,950		969	697	512	386	238	160
2,000		981	703	515	388	239	160
2,500		1088	756	543	404	245	162
3,000		1173	796	563	415	249	164
3,500		1242	827	579	423	252	166
4,000		1300	852	591	430	254	166
4,300		1330	865	597	433	255	167
4,400	2183	1339	869	599	434	255	167
4,500	2207	1348	873	601	435	256	167
5,000	2321	1390	890	609	439	257	168
7,500	2745	1532	946	635	453	262	170
10,000	3022	1614	977	648	459	264	171
12,500	3216	1668	997	657	464	265	171
15,000	3360	1706	1010	663	467	266	172
20,000	3560	1756	1027	670	470	267	172
30,000	3784	1809	1045	678	474	269	173
40,000	3907	1836	1054	682	476	269	173
50,000	3985	1853	1060	684	477	270	173
100,000	4150	1888	1071	688	479	270	173
200,000	4238	1906	1077	691	480	271	174
300,000	4269	1913	1079	692	481	271	174
500,000	4293	1917	1081	692	481	271	174

Table D.1e. Sample sizes for sampling attributes for random samples only. Expected rate of occurrence not over 30 percent or expected rate of occurrence not less than 70 percent. Confidence level 90 percent (two-sided).

Population size	Sample size for precision of					
	±1%	±2%	±3%	±4%	±5%	±7%
250					120	80
300					130	84
350					138	88
400				189	145	90
450				199	152	93
500				208	157	95
550				216	161	96
600				224	165	98
650			321	230	169	99
700			332	236	172	100
750			343	242	175	101
800			353	246	178	102
850			363	251	180	103
900			372	255	182	103
950			380	259	184	104
1,000			388	263	186	104
1,250			420	277	193	107
1,400			436	284	196	108
1,450		718	440	286	197	108
1,500		730	445	288	198	108
2,000		831	480	302	205	110
2,500		906	505	311	205	111
3,000		965	522	318	212	112
3,500		1011	535	323	214	113
4,000		1045	546	327	216	113
4,500		1080	554	330	217	114
5,000		1107	561	332	218	114
6,000	2919	1149	572	336	220	114
7,500	3234	1195	583	340	221	115
10,000	3624	1244	594	343	223	115
15,000	4122	1298	606	347	224	116
20,000	4426	1328	613	349	225	116
30,000	4778	1357	619	352	226	116
40,000	4976	1372	622	353	227	116
50,000	5103	1382	624	353	227	116
60,000	5192	1388	625	354	227	116
70,000	5256	1393	626	354	227	116
80,000	5306	1396	627	354	227	116
90,000	5346	1399	628	354	227	116
100,000	5378	1401	628	354	227	116
150,000	5476	1408	629	355	227	116
200,000	5526	1411	630	355	228	116
300,000	5578	1414	631	355	228	116
400,000	5604	1416	631	355	228	116
500,000	5619	1417	631	355	228	116

Table D.1f. Sample sizes for sampling attributes for random samples only. Expected rate of occurrence not over 40 percent or expected rate of occurrence not less than 60 percent. Confidence level 90 percent (two-sided).

Population size	Sample size for precision of					
	±1%	±2%	±3%	±4%	±5%	±7%
100						57
200						80
300					140	92
400				202	158	100
500				225	171	105
600				243	182	109
650				250	186	111
700			356	257	190	112
750			368	264	193	113
800			380	270	197	114
850			391	275	199	115
900			401	280	202	116
950			411	285	204	117
1,000			420	289	207	118
1,250			458	307	216	120
1,550			493	322	223	123
1,600		807	498	324	224	123
1,750		843	511	330	227	124
2,000		897	531	338	230	125
2,500		985	560	350	236	126
3,000		1054	582	358	240	127
3,500		1110	599	364	242	128
4,000		1155	612	369	244	129
4,500		1194	622	373	246	129
5,000		1226	631	376	247	130
7,500	3481	1335	659	386	252	131
10,000	3938	1397	674	391	254	131
15,000	4533	1466	689	396	256	132
20,000	4903	1502	697	398	257	132
30,000	5339	1541	705	401	258	132
40,000	5588	1561	709	402	259	133
50,000	5748	1573	712	403	259	133
60,000	5861	1581	714	404	259	133
70,000	5944	1587	715	404	259	133
80,000	6007	1592	716	404	259	133
90,000	6058	1595	716	405	260	133
100,000	6099	1598	717	405	260	133
150,000	6225	1607	719	405	260	133
200,000	6291	1611	720	406	260	133
300,000	6357	1615	720	406	260	133
400,000	6391	1618	721	406	260	133
500,000	6412	1619	721	406	260	133

Table D.1g. Sample sizes for sampling attributes for random samples only. Expected rate of occurrence of 50 percent. Confidence level 90 percent (two-sided).

Population size	Sample size for precision of					
	±1%	±2%	±3%	±4%	±5%	±7%
250					130	89
300					143	95
350					153	100
400					162	103
450				218	169	106
500				230	176	109
550				240	182	111
600				249	187	113
650				257	192	114
700				264	196	116
750				271	199	117
800			388	277	203	118
850			399	283	206	119
900			410	288	209	120
950			420	293	211	121
1,000			430	298	213	122
1,500			501	330	230	127
1,650			517	337	233	128
1,700		848	522	339	234	128
2,000		917	547	350	239	130
2,500		1009	578	362	245	131
3,000		1082	602	371	249	132
3,500		1141	619	378	252	133
4,000		1189	633	383	254	134
4,500		1230	645	387	256	134
5,000		1264	654	390	257	135
6,500		1343	674	397	260	136
7,000	3441	1363	679	399	261	136
8,000	3666	1397	688	402	262	136
10,000	4036	1447	700	406	264	137
15,000	4663	1520	716	412	266	137
20,000	5056	1560	725	415	267	138
30,000	5521	1602	734	417	269	138
40,000	5787	1623	738	419	269	138
50,000	5959	1636	741	420	270	138
60,000	6080	1645	743	420	270	138
70,000	6169	1652	744	421	270	138
80,000	6238	1657	745	421	270	138
90,000	6293	1661	746	421	270	138
100,000	6337	1664	747	422	270	138
150,000	6474	1673	748	422	271	138
200,000	6544	1678	749	422	271	138
300,000	6616	1682	750	423	271	138
400,000	6653	1685	751	423	271	139
500,000	6675	1686	751	423	271	139

Table D.2a. Sample sizes for sampling attributes for random samples only. Expected rate of occurrence not over 2 percent or expected rate of occurrence not less than 98 percent. Confidence level 95 percent (two-sided).

Population size	Sample size for precision of					
	±.5%	±.75%	±1%	±1.25%	±1.5%	±2%
200						97
250						108
300						116
350					172	123
400					182	129
450					192	133
500				246	201	137
550				257	209	141
600				268	215	144
650				277	221	146
700				286	227	149
750				294	232	151
800				301	236	153
850				308	241	155
900				314	244	156
950				320	248	158
1,000			430	326	251	159
1,300			477	352	267	165
1,350		673	484	356	269	166
1,500		708	501	365	274	168
2,000		802	547	389	287	173
2,500		872	579	405	296	176
3,000		925	602	416	302	178
3,100	1528	935	606	418	303	178
3,500	1619	969	620	424	306	179
4,000	1719	1003	634	431	309	180
4,500	1805	1032	645	436	312	181
5,000	1880	1056	654	440	314	182
7,500	2149	1136	685	453	320	184
10,000	2315	1181	700	460	324	185
15,000	2509	1229	717	467	328	186
20,000	2619	1255	726	471	330	187
30,000	2738	1282	735	475	331	188
40,000	2801	1296	740	477	332	188
50,000	2841	1304	742	478	333	188
60,000	2868	1310	744	479	333	188
70,000	2888	1314	745	479	334	188
80,000	2903	1317	746	480	334	188
90,000	2915	1319	747	480	334	188
100,000	2925	1321	747	480	334	188
150,000	2953	1327	750	481	334	189
200,000	2968	1330	751	481	335	189
300,000	2982	1333	752	482	335	189
400,000	2990	1335	752	482	335	189
500,000	2994	1336	752	482	335	189

Table D.2b. Sample sizes for sampling attributes for random samples only. Expected rate of occurrence not over 5 percent or expected rate of occurrence not less than 95 percent. Confidence level 95 percent (two-sided).

Population size	Sample size for precision of						
	±.5%	±1%	±1.5%	±2%	±2.5%	±3%	±4%
150							65
200							73
250						112	79
300					148	121	83
350					160	129	86
400					169	135	89
450					178	140	91
500				239	185	144	93
550				250	191	148	95
600				259	197	152	96
650				268	202	155	97
700				276	207	157	98
750				284	211	160	99
800				291	214	162	100
850			416	297	218	164	101
900			427	303	221	166	101
950			438	308	224	167	102
1,000			448	314	226	169	102
1,200			484	331	235	174	104
1,500			527	350	245	179	106
1,750			555	362	251	182	107
1,800		907	560	364	252	182	107
2,000		954	578	372	255	184	108
2,200		998	593	378	258	186	108
2,500		1055	613	386	262	188	109
3,000		1135	639	396	267	190	110
3,500		1200	659	404	270	192	110
4,000		1253	675	410	273	193	111
4,500		1299	688	414	275	194	111
5,000		1337	698	418	276	195	112
7,000		1448	727	428	281	197	112
7,500	3700	1468	732	430	282	197	112
8,000	3817	1486	737	432	282	198	112
9,000	4031	1517	744	434	283	198	113
10,000	4220	1543	751	436	284	199	113
15,000	4851	1627	770	443	287	200	113
20,000	5348	1672	780	446	288	201	113
30,000	5871	1720	790	449	290	201	114
40,000	6173	1745	795	451	290	202	114
50,000	6370	1761	799	452	291	202	114
100,000	6803	1792	805	454	292	202	114
200,000	7043	1809	808	455	292	203	114
300,000	7126	1814	809	456	292	203	114
400,000	7169	1817	810	456	292	203	114
500,000	7196	1818	810	456	292	203	114

Table D.2c. Sample sizes for sampling attributes for random samples only. Expected rate of occurrence not over 10 percent or expected rate of occurrence not less than 90 percent. Confidence level 95 percent (two-sided).

Population size	Sample size for precision of						
	±.5%	±1%	±1.5%	±2%	±2.5%	±3%	±4%
250							116
300							126
350							134
400						196	141
450						207	146
500						217	151
550						226	155
600					283	234	159
650					299	242	162
700					309	248	165
750					319	254	168
800					328	260	170
850					336	265	172
900				441	343	269	174
950				453	350	274	176
1,000				464	357	278	178
1,500				549	405	306	189
1,550			772	555	408	308	190
1,750			819	579	421	315	192
2,000			869	604	434	322	195
2,500			952	641	453	333	199
3,000			1020	671	468	341	202
3,400			1062	689	476	345	203
3,500		1739	1068	693	478	346	204
4,000		1855	1111	711	486	351	205
4,500		1955	1146	725	493	354	206
5,000		2044	1176	737	499	357	207
6,000		2194	1224	756	507	361	209
7,000		2314	1261	769	513	364	210
8,000		2414	1290	780	518	367	210
9,000		2493	1313	789	522	368	211
10,000		2569	1332	796	525	370	212
13,500		2752	1380	812	532	374	213
14,000	6957	2773	1385	814	533	374	213
15,000	7196	2810	1394	817	534	375	213
20,000	8176	2948	1427	828	539	377	214
30,000	9465	3100	1462	840	544	379	215
40,000	10277	3182	1480	846	546	380	215
50,000	10834	3234	1491	850	548	381	215
75,000	11677	3305	1506	854	550	382	215
100,000	12150	3242	1514	857	551	383	216
150,000	12663	3379	1522	859	552	383	216
200,000	12936	3398	1525	861	552	383	216
350,000	13303	3423	1530	862	553	384	216
500,000	13459	3433	1532	863	553	384	216

Table D.2d. Sample sizes for sampling attributes for random samples only. Expected rate of occurrence not over 20 percent or expected rate of occurrence not less than 80 percent. Confidence level 95 percent (two-sided).

Population size	Sample size for precision of						
	±1%	±1.5%	±2%	±2.5%	±3%	±4%	±5%
400						196	153
450						207	159
500						218	165
550						226	170
600						234	175
650						242	179
700					346	248	182
750					358	254	185
800					369	260	188
850					379	265	191
900					389	269	193
950					398	274	195
1,000				496	406	278	198
1,250				551	442	294	206
1,500				595	470	306	211
1,550			772	602	474	308	212
1,750			818	630	491	315	216
2,000			869	660	509	322	219
2,500			952	706	537	333	224
2,800		1383	992	728	549	338	226
2,900		1407	1005	735	553	339	227
3,500		1535	1068	768	572	346	230
4,000		1624	1110	790	584	351	232
4,500		1700	1146	808	593	354	233
5,000		1767	1176	822	601	357	234
6,000		1878	1224	845	613	361	236
6,500	3160	1924	1243	855	618	363	237
7,500	3378	2003	1276	870	626	366	238
8,500	3567	2068	1302	882	632	368	239
10,000	3807	2146	1332	896	639	370	240
12,500	4121	2242	1369	912	648	373	241
15,000	4360	2311	1394	923	653	375	242
17,500	4549	2363	1413	932	657	376	242
20,000	4702	2404	1427	938	660	377	243
30,000	5102	2504	1462	953	668	379	244
40,000	5328	2558	1480	960	672	381	244
50,000	5474	2591	1491	965	674	381	245
60,000	5576	2613	1498	968	675	382	245
70,000	5651	2630	1504	970	676	382	245
80,000	5708	2642	1508	972	677	382	245
90,000	5754	2652	1511	973	678	383	245
100,000	5791	2660	1514	974	678	383	245
200,000	5964	2696	1525	979	681	383	246
300,000	6024	2708	1529	981	682	384	246
500,000	6072	2717	1532	982	682	384	246

Table D.2e. Sample sizes for sampling attributes for random samples only. Expected rate of occurrence not over 30 percent or expected rate of occurrence not less than 70 percent. Confidence level 95 percent (two-sided).

Population size	Sample size for precision of					
	±1%	±2%	±3%	±4%	±5%	±7%
450					188	121
550				263	204	127
650				284	216	132
800				310	230	137
850				317	234	138
950			461	330	241	141
1,000			473	335	244	142
1,300			531	363	259	147
1,500			561	378	266	149
1,800			599	394	274	151
2,000			619	403	278	153
2,100		1,029	628	407	280	153
2,500		1117	660	420	286	155
3,000		1206	690	432	291	157
3,500		1280	714	441	296	158
4,000		1341	732	448	299	159
4,500		1393	748	453	301	159
5,000		1437	760	458	303	160
6,000		1510	780	465	306	161
7,000		1566	795	470	309	161
8,000		1611	806	474	310	162
8,500	4139	1630	811	476	311	162
9,000	4254	1648	815	477	312	162
10,000	4465	1678	823	480	313	162
12,500	4903	1737	836	485	315	163
15,000	5246	1778	846	488	316	163
17,500	5522	1808	853	490	317	164
20,000	5749	1832	858	492	318	164
25,000	6099	1866	865	494	319	164
30,000	6358	1890	870	496	319	164
40,000	6713	1920	877	498	320	164
50,000	6946	1939	881	499	321	165
60,000	7111	1951	883	500	321	165
70,000	7233	1960	885	501	321	165
80,000	7328	1967	886	501	321	165
90,000	7403	1973	888	501	322	165
100,000	7465	1977	888	502	322	165
150,000	7655	1990	891	503	322	165
200,000	7754	1997	892	503	322	165
300,000	7856	2003	894	503	322	165
400,000	7908	2007	894	504	322	165
500,000	7939	2009	895	504	322	165

Table D.2f. Sample sizes for sampling attributes for random samples only. Expected rate of occurrence not over 40% or expected rate of occurrence not less than 60%. Confidence level 95% (two-sided).

Population size	Sample size for precision of					
	±1%	±2%	±3%	±4%	±5%	±7%
500					213	137
600				294	229	144
700				316	242	149
850				344	258	155
1,000				366	262	159
1,050			519	372	273	160
1,500			609	417	297	168
2,000			678	448	312	172
2,200			699	457	316	174
2,400		1176	718	465	320	175
2,500		1200	727	468	322	175
3,000		1304	764	484	329	178
3,400		1374	787	493	333	179
4,000		1463	816	504	338	180
5,000		1578	850	517	344	182
6,000		1665	875	526	348	183
7,500		1763	901	535	352	184
9,000		1835	920	542	355	185
9,500	4679	1855	925	543	356	185
10,000	4797	1873	929	545	356	185
12,500	5306	1946	947	551	359	186
15,000	5710	1998	959	555	360	186
17,500	6039	2037	968	558	362	187
20,000	6311	2067	975	560	363	187
25,000	6736	2110	984	563	364	187
30,000	7053	2141	991	565	365	187
40,000	7493	2179	999	568	366	188
50,000	7785	2203	1004	570	367	188
60,000	7992	2220	1007	571	367	188
70,000	8147	2232	1010	572	367	188
80,000	8267	2240	1012	572	368	188
90,000	8363	2247	1013	573	368	188
100,000	8442	2253	1014	573	368	188
110,000	8507	2258	1015	573	368	188
120,000	8562	2262	1016	574	368	188
130,000	8609	2265	1016	574	368	188
140,000	8651	2268	1017	574	368	188
150,000	8686	2271	1018	574	368	188
200,000	8814	2279	1019	575	369	188
300,000	8945	2288	1021	575	369	189
400,000	9013	2292	1022	576	369	189
500,000	9053	2294	1023	576	369	189

Table D.2g. Sample sizes for sampling attributes for random samples only. Expected rate of occurrence 50 percent. Confidence level 95 percent (two-sided).

Population size	Sample size for precision of					
	±1%	±2%	±3%	±4%	±5%	±7%
500					217	141
600				300	234	148
700				323	248	154
800				343	260	158
950				368	274	163
1,000				375	278	164
1,100			542	389	285	167
1,200			565	400	291	169
1,300			586	411	297	171
1,400			606	420	302	172
1,500			624	429	306	174
1,850			677	453	318	178
2,100			708	467	325	180
2,300			729	476	329	181
2,500		1225	748	484	333	182
3,000		1334	787	500	341	184
3,400		1407	812	510	345	186
4,000		1501	843	522	351	187
5,000		1622	880	536	357	189
6,000		1715	906	546	361	190
7,000		1788	926	553	364	191
8,000		1847	942	558	367	192
9,500		1917	959	565	369	193
10,000	4899	1936	964	566	370	193
12,500	5431	2014	983	573	373	193
15,000	5855	2070	996	577	375	194
17,500	6201	2111	1006	580	376	194
20,000	6489	2144	1013	583	377	195
30,000	7275	2223	1030	588	379	195
40,000	7745	2265	1039	591	381	196
50,000	8057	2291	1045	593	381	196
60,000	8279	2309	1048	594	382	196
70,000	8445	2321	1051	595	382	196
80,000	8575	2331	1053	596	382	196
90,000	8678	2339	1055	596	383	196
100,000	8763	2345	1056	597	383	196
125,000	8919	2356	1058	597	383	196
150,000	9026	2363	1060	598	383	196
200,000	9164	2373	1061	598	383	196
300,000	9306	2382	1063	599	384	196
400,000	9379	2387	1064	599	384	196
500,000	9423	2390	1065	600	384	196

Table D.3a. Sample sizes for sampling attributes for random samples only. Expected rate of occurrence not over 2 percent or expected rate of occurrence not less than 98 percent. Confidence level 99 percent (two-sided).

Population size	Sample size for precision of					
	±.5%	±.75%	±1%	±1.25%	±1.5%	±2%
400						180
450						189
500						197
550						205
600					295	211
650					306	217
700					317	222
750					327	227
800				408	336	232
850				421	344	236
900				433	352	239
1,000				455	367	246
1,250				500	396	258
1,300			650	508	400	260
1,500			697	536	418	268
1,750			746	564	435	275
2,000			788	587	449	280
2,200			818	604	458	284
2,300		1153	831	611	462	285
2,500		1201	856	625	470	288
3,000		1306	907	652	485	294
3,500		1392	948	673	496	298
4,000		1465	981	689	505	301
4,000		1527	1009	702	512	304
5,000		1581	1032	714	518	306
5,500	2673	1627	1052	723	523	307
7,500	3071	1767	1108	749	537	312
10,000	3421	1877	1151	768	547	315
12,500	3672	1950	1178	780	553	317
15,000	3861	2003	1197	789	557	319
17,500	4008	2041	1210	795	560	319
20,000	4126	2072	1221	799	562	320
30,000	4431	2146	1246	810	567	322
40,000	4601	2185	1259	815	570	323
50,000	4709	2209	1267	819	572	323
60,000	4784	2225	1273	821	573	324
70,000	4839	2237	1276	822	573	324
80,000	4883	2246	1279	824	574	324
90,000	4916	2253	1282	825	574	324
100,000	4942	2259	1283	825	575	324
150,000	5025	2276	1289	828	576	325
200,000	5067	2285	1292	829	576	325
300,000	5110	2293	1294	830	577	325
400,000	5132	2298	1296	831	577	325
500,000	5145	2300	1297	831	577	325

Table D.3b. Sample sizes for sampling attributes for random samples only. Expected rate of occurrence not over 5 percent or expected rate of occurrence not less than 95 percent. Confidence level 99 percent (two-sided).

Population size	Sample size for precision of						
	±.5%	±1%	±1.5%	±2%	±2.5%	±3%	±4%
200							99
250							110
300							119
350						175	126
400						187	132
450						197	137
500						206	142
550					263	214	145
600					274	221	148
650					284	228	151
700					293	234	154
750					302	239	156
800				397	310	244	158
850				409	318	248	160
900				420	324	252	162
1,000				441	336	260	165
1,250				484	360	274	170
1,350				498	367	278	172
1,400			700	504	371	280	173
1,500			725	517	378	284	174
1,750			778	544	392	292	177
2,000			824	565	403	298	179
2,500			898	599	420	307	183
3,100			965	628	434	315	185
3,200		1588	974	632	436	316	186
3,500		1659	1000	643	441	318	187
4,000		1763	1037	658	448	322	188
4,400		1837	1062	668	452	324	189
5,000		1934	1094	681	458	327	190
7,500		2220	1180	713	473	335	192
10,000		2397	1228	731	480	338	193
12,000		2496	1254	740	484	340	194
12,500	6274	2517	1259	741	485	341	194
15,000	6847	2605	1281	749	488	342	194
20,000	7730	2721	1309	758	492	344	195
30,000	8873	2851	1338	768	496	346	196
40,000	9581	2920	1353	773	498	347	196
50,000	10063	2963	1362	776	499	348	196
80,000	10884	3033	1376	780	501	349	197
100,000	11189	3056	1381	782	502	349	197
150,000	11623	3085	1387	784	503	349	197
200,000	11852	3101	1391	785	503	350	197
250,000	11994	3111	1393	785	503	350	197
375,000	12189	3124	1395	786	504	350	197
500,000	12289	3132	1396	787	504	350	197

Table D.3c. Sample sizes for sampling attributes for random samples only. Expected rate of occurrence not over 10 percent or expected rate of occurrence not less than 90 percent. Confidence level 99 percent (two-sided).

Population size	Sample size for precision of						
	±.5%	±1%	±1.5%	±2%	±2.5%	±3%	±4%
400							193
450							204
500							214
550							223
600							230
650							237
700						341	244
750						352	249
800						363	255
850						373	260
900						382	264
950						391	268
1,000					489	399	272
1,250					542	434	288
1,450					576	455	297
1,500				748	584	460	299
1,750				806	618	481	308
2,000				855	647	498	315
2,500				935	691	525	325
2,600				949	699	529	327
2,700			1338	962	706	533	328
3,000			1407	997	725	544	332
3,500			1508	1047	751	558	337
4,000			1595	1087	771	569	341
4,500			1669	1121	788	578	345
5,000			1733	1150	802	586	347
7,500		3325	1960	1245	847	610	356
10,000		3739	2097	1299	872	622	360
12,500		4041	2189	1334	888	630	362
15,000		4272	2254	1358	898	635	364
17,500		4453	2304	1376	906	639	365
20,000		4599	2342	1389	912	642	366
30,000	13294	4981	2437	1422	926	649	369
40,000	14950	5193	2488	1439	933	653	370
50,000	16157	5332	2519	1450	937	655	371
60,000	17075	5431	2540	1457	940	656	371
70,000	17798	5503	2556	1462	942	657	371
80,000	18385	5557	2568	1466	944	658	372
90,000	18867	5600	2577	1469	945	659	372
100,000	19269	5636	2584	1471	946	659	372
150,000	20594	5740	2607	1478	949	661	372
200,000	21326	5795	2618	1481	951	661	373
300,000	22111	5852	2630	1485	952	662	373
450,000	22526	5880	2635	1487	953	662	373
500,000	22786	5902	2639	1489	953	663	373

Table D.3d. Sample sizes for sampling attributes for random samples only. Expected rate of occurrence not over 20 percent or expected rate of occurrence not less than 80 percent. Confidence level 95 percent (two-sided).

Population size	Sample size for precision of						
	±1%	±1.5%	±2%	±2.5%	±3%	±4%	±5%
450							219
500							230
550							240
600							249
650							257
700						341	265
750						352	271
800						363	278
850						373	283
900						382	289
1,000						399	298
1,050						407	303
1,100						414	307
1,150						421	310
1,200					595	428	314
1,250					607	434	317
1,500					661	460	331
1,650					688	473	338
1,700				850	697	477	340
2,000				919	742	498	350
2,600				1027	812	529	365
2,700			1339	1043	821	533	367
3,000			1409	1085	847	544	372
3,500			1510	1144	882	558	379
4,000			1596	1192	911	569	384
4,600			1683	1240	939	580	389
4,700		2354	1697	1248	943	586	390
5,000		2427	1734	1268	955	598	392
6,000		2641	1840	1324	986	606	397
7,000		2818	1925	1367	1010	613	400
8,000		2967	1993	1401	1028	613	403
9,000		3095	2050	1429	1043	618	406
10,000		3204	2098	1452	1055	622	407
10,500		3254	2119	1462	1061	624	408
11,000	5403	3301	2138	1471	1065	626	409
15,000	6217	3588	2255	1525	1094	635	413
20,000	6936	3816	2343	1565	1114	642	416
30,000	7842	4075	2439	1607	1135	649	419
40,000	8390	4218	2489	1629	1146	653	420
50,000	8758	4309	2520	1642	1152	655	421
75,000	9301	4437	2564	1660	1161	658	422
100,000	9598	4503	2586	1670	1166	659	423
200,000	10082	4607	2619	1684	1173	661	424
350,000	10304	4653	2634	1690	1176	662	424
500,000	10396	4672	2640	1692	1177	663	424

Table D.3e. Sample sizes for sampling attributes for random samples only. Expected rate of occurrence not over 30 percent or expected rate of occurrence not less than 70 percent. Confidence level 99 percent (two-sided).

Population size	Sample size for precision of					
	±1%	±2%	±3%	±4%	±5%	±7%
600					289	193
700					311	203
800					329	210
900					344	216
950				455	352	219
1,050				476	364	224
1,300				522	390	234
1,500				551	407	239
1,600			787	564	414	242
2,000			873	607	436	249
2,400			941	639	452	255
2,600			971	653	459	257
3,000			1021	675	470	260
3,400			1064	693	479	263
3,500		1746	1074	698	481	263
4,000		1862	1116	715	489	266
4,500		1964	1152	730	496	268
5,000		2053	1182	742	502	269
6,500		2268	1251	768	513	273
7,500		2379	1284	780	519	274
8,500		2471	1310	790	523	275
10,000		2584	1341	801	528	277
12,000		2700	1371	812	533	278
13,500		2769	1389	818	535	279
14,000	6984	2790	1394	820	536	279
15,000	7224	2827	1404	823	537	279
17,500	7753	2906	1423	830	540	280
20,000	8213	2967	1437	835	542	281
25,000	8948	3058	1458	842	545	281
30,000	9515	3121	1472	846	547	282
40,000	10335	3205	1491	852	550	283
50,000	10898	3257	1502	856	551	283
60,000	11309	3293	1509	858	552	283
70,000	11622	3319	1515	860	553	284
80,000	11868	3338	1519	862	554	284
90,000	12067	3354	1522	863	554	284
100,000	12231	3367	1525	863	554	284
150,000	12751	3405	1533	866	555	284
200,000	13027	3424	1536	867	556	284
300,000	13316	3444	1540	868	556	284
400,000	13466	3454	1542	869	557	284
500,000	13557	3460	1544	869	557	285

Table D.3f. Sample sizes for sampling attributes for random samples only. Expected rate of occurrence not over 40 percent or expected rate of occurrence not less than 60 percent. Confidence level 99 percent (two-sided).

Population size	Sample size for precision of					
	±1%	±2%	±3%	±4%	±5%	±7%
1,000				499	389	245
1,200				544	416	256
1,500				599	447	267
1,750				635	467	274
1,800			893	641	471	276
2,000			939	665	483	280
2,200			981	686	494	283
2,500			1036	712	508	288
2,800			1085	735	519	292
3,000			1113	748	526	294
3,400			1164	770	537	297
3,800			1208	789	546	300
4,000		1996	1227	797	550	301
4,200		2044	1245	805	553	302
4,500		2113	1270	815	558	303
4,800		2177	1293	825	563	305
5,000		2217	1307	830	565	305
6,500		2469	1391	863	580	310
7,500		2601	1432	879	587	312
8,500		2712	1465	891	593	313
10,000		2848	1504	905	599	315
12,500		3020	1550	922	606	317
15,000		3147	1583	933	611	318
15,500		3168	1588	935	612	319
16,000	7982	3188	1593	937	613	319
17,500	8338	3244	1607	942	615	319
18,500	8559	3277	1615	945	616	320
20,000	8866	3321	1626	948	617	320
25,000	9729	3435	1653	957	621	321
30,000	10403	3515	1671	963	624	322
35,000	10946	3575	1684	968	626	322
40,000	11391	3621	1695	971	627	323
45,000	11763	3658	1703	974	628	323
50,000	12079	3688	1709	976	629	323
60,000	12586	3734	1719	979	630	324
70,000	12974	3767	1726	981	631	324
80,000	13282	3793	1731	983	632	324
90,000	13532	3813	1735	984	633	324
100,000	13738	3829	1739	986	633	324
120,000	14060	3854	1744	987	634	324
150,000	14397	3879	1749	989	634	325
200,000	14751	3904	1754	990	635	325
300,000	15123	3929	1759	992	636	325
400,000	15316	3942	1762	993	636	325
500,000	15434	3950	1763	993	636	325

Table D.3g. Sample sizes for sampling attributes for random samples only. Expected rate of occurrence 50 percent. Confidence level 99 percent (two-sided).

Population size	Sample size for precision of					
	±1%	±2%	±3%	±4%	±5%	±7%
1,050				522	407	256
1,250				567	434	267
1,500				613	460	277
1,650				637	473	281
1,800				658	485	285
1,850			924	665	489	286
2,000			959	683	498	290
2,200			1003	705	510	294
2,400			1043	724	520	297
2,500			1061	733	525	298
3,000			1142	771	544	305
3,400			1195	795	555	308
3,600			1219	805	560	310
4,000			1262	824	569	312
4,100		2062	1272	828	571	313
4,300		2111	1290	836	575	314
4,500		2158	1308	843	578	315
4,700		2203	1324	850	582	316
5,000		2267	1347	859	586	317
6,500		2532	1436	894	602	322
7,500		2671	1480	911	610	324
8,500		2788	1515	924	616	326
10,000		2932	1556	939	622	328
12,500		3114	1606	957	630	330
14,000		3200	1629	965	634	331
15,000		3249	1642	970	635	331
16,500		3314	1658	976	638	332
17,000	8396	3334	1663	977	639	332
18,500	8746	3388	1676	982	641	333
20,000	9068	3435	1688	986	642	333
25,000	9972	3557	1717	996	646	334
30,000	10682	3644	1737	1002	649	335
35,000	11255	3708	1751	1007	651	336
40,000	11726	3758	1762	1011	653	336
45,000	12121	3797	1771	1013	654	336
50,000	12456	3830	1778	1016	655	337
75,000	13584	3930	1799	1023	658	337
80,000	13740	3943	1802	1024	658	337
100,000	14229	3982	1810	1026	659	338
125,000	14645	4014	1816	1028	660	338
150,000	14937	4036	1821	1030	661	338
200,000	15318	4063	1826	1031	661	338
300,000	15720	4091	1832	1033	662	338
400,000	15928	4105	1835	1034	662	339
500,000	16056	4113	1836	1035	663	339

Tables for Probabilities of Including at Least One Occurrence in a Sample for Discovery Sampling

Source: Herbert Arkin, *Handbook of Sampling for Auditing and Accounting*, 3d ed. Englewood Cliffs, N.J.: Prentice Hall (a division of Simon & Schuster), 1984. Used with permission.

Table E.1a. Probabilities of including at least one occurrence in a sample (discovery sampling)

Probability level 85%
Sample size when occurrence rate is

Field size	0.1	0.2	0.3	0.4	0.5	0.6	0.7	0.8	0.9	1.0	1.5	2.0	2.5	3.0	4.0	5.0
200	200	198	192	181	170	159	148	139	130	123	94	76	63	54	42	35
300	299	287	264	238	215	195	178	164	151	141	103	81	67	57	44	36
400	397	363	318	278	245	219	197	179	164	151	108	84	69	58	45	36
500	489	425	359	306	266	234	209	189	172	158	112	86	70	59	45	37
600	575	477	391	328	281	246	218	196	178	163	114	88	71	60	46	37
700	653	519	416	344	293	254	225	201	182	166	116	89	72	60	46	37
800	725	556	437	358	302	261	230	205	185	169	117	89	72	61	46	37
900	791	586	454	369	310	267	234	208	188	171	118	90	73	61	46	37
1000	850	613	469	378	316	271	237	211	190	173	119	90	73	61	46	37
1500	1077	703	516	407	335	285	248	219	197	178	121	92	74	62	47	38
2000	1225	755	542	422	346	292	253	224	200	181	123	93	74	62	47	38
2500	1329	789	559	432	352	297	257	226	202	183	123	93	75	62	47	38
3000	1406	813	570	439	356	300	259	228	204	184	124	93	75	63	47	38
4000	1511	844	585	447	362	304	262	230	205	185	124	94	75	63	47	38
5000	1579	864	594	452	365	306	264	232	206	186	125	94	75	63	47	38
6000	1626	877	600	456	368	308	265	233	207	187	125	94	75	63	47	38
7000	1662	887	605	459	369	309	266	233	208	187	125	94	76	63	47	38
8000	1689	894	608	460	371	310	266	234	208	187	126	94	76	63	47	38
9000	1711	900	611	462	372	311	267	234	208	188	126	94	76	63	47	38
10000	1728	905	613	463	372	311	267	234	209	188	126	94	76	63	47	38
15000	1782	919	619	467	375	313	269	235	209	188	126	94	76	63	47	38
20000	1810	926	622	469	376	314	269	236	210	189	126	95	76	63	47	38
25000	1827	931	624	470	377	314	270	236	210	189	126	95	76	63	47	38
30000	1838	934	626	471	377	315	270	236	210	189	126	95	76	63	47	38
35000	1847	936	627	471	377	315	270	236	210	189	126	95	76	63	47	38
40000	1853	937	627	471	378	315	270	236	210	189	126	95	76	63	47	38
45000	1858	939	628	472	378	315	270	237	210	189	126	95	76	63	47	38
50000	1862	940	628	472	378	315	270	237	210	189	126	95	76	63	47	38

Table E.2a. Probabilities of including at least one occurrence in a sample (discovery sampling)

Probability level 90%
Sample size when occurrence rate is

Field size	0.1	0.2	0.3	0.4	0.5	0.6	0.7	0.8	0.9	1.0	1.5	2.0	2.5	3.0	4.0	5.0
200	200	199	196	189	180	171	161	153	144	137	107	88	74	64	50	41
300	300	294	277	256	235	217	200	185	172	161	120	96	79	68	52	43
400	399	378	341	305	274	247	224	205	189	175	127	100	82	70	54	43
500	495	450	392	342	301	268	241	219	200	185	132	103	84	71	54	44
600	587	512	433	370	322	284	253	229	208	191	135	105	85	72	55	44
700	674	565	466	392	337	295	262	236	214	196	138	106	86	73	55	45
800	755	610	494	410	350	305	270	242	219	200	140	107	87	73	56	45
900	830	650	516	425	360	312	276	246	223	203	141	108	88	74	56	45
1000	900	684	536	438	369	319	280	250	226	206	142	109	88	74	56	45
1500	1177	804	601	478	397	339	295	262	235	213	146	111	89	75	56	45
2000	1368	875	637	500	411	349	303	268	240	217	148	112	90	75	57	46
2500	1505	923	661	514	421	356	308	272	243	220	149	113	90	76	57	46
3000	1608	956	677	524	427	360	312	274	245	222	150	113	91	76	57	46
4000	1751	1000	698	536	435	366	316	278	248	224	151	113	91	76	57	46
5000	1845	1028	712	544	440	369	318	280	249	225	151	114	91	76	57	46
6000	1912	1048	720	549	443	372	320	281	250	226	152	114	91	76	57	46
7000	1962	1062	727	553	446	373	321	282	251	227	152	114	92	76	57	46
8000	2001	1072	732	555	448	375	322	283	252	227	152	114	92	76	57	46
9000	2032	1081	736	558	449	376	323	283	252	227	152	114	92	76	57	46
10000	2057	1087	739	559	450	376	324	284	253	228	152	114	92	76	57	46
15000	2135	1108	748	565	454	379	325	285	254	229	153	115	92	77	57	46
20000	2175	1119	753	567	455	380	326	286	254	229	153	115	92	77	57	46
25000	2200	1125	756	569	456	381	327	286	255	229	153	115	92	77	58	46
30000	2216	1129	758	570	457	381	327	286	255	229	153	115	92	77	58	46
35000	2228	1133	759	571	458	382	327	287	255	230	153	115	92	77	58	46
40000	2238	1135	760	572	458	382	328	287	255	230	153	115	92	77	58	46
45000	2245	1137	761	572	458	382	328	287	255	230	153	115	92	77	58	46
50000	2250	1138	762	572	458	382	328	287	255	230	153	115	92	77	58	46

Table E.3a. Probabilities of including at least one occurrence in a sample (discovery sampling)

Probability level 95%
Sample size when occurrence rate is

Field size	0.1	0.2	0.3	0.4	0.5	0.6	0.7	0.8	0.9	1.0	1.5	2.0	2.5	3.0	4.0	5.0
200	200	200	199	195	190	184	176	169	162	155	126	105	90	79	62	52
300	300	298	289	275	259	243	228	214	201	189	146	118	99	85	66	54
400	400	391	367	338	311	285	263	243	226	211	157	125	104	88	68	56
500	499	475	432	388	349	316	288	264	243	225	165	129	107	91	70	56
600	596	551	486	428	379	339	306	279	255	236	170	133	109	92	70	57
700	690	618	532	460	403	357	320	290	265	244	174	135	110	93	71	57
800	781	677	570	486	422	371	331	299	272	250	177	137	111	94	71	58
900	868	730	603	508	437	383	341	306	278	255	179	138	112	95	72	58
1000	950	776	632	527	451	393	348	312	283	259	181	139	113	95	72	58
1500	1296	947	729	590	494	425	372	331	299	272	187	143	115	97	73	59
2000	1553	1054	786	625	518	442	385	341	307	278	190	144	116	97	74	59
2500	1746	1127	823	647	533	453	393	348	312	282	192	145	117	98	74	59
3000	1895	1179	849	663	543	460	399	352	315	285	193	146	117	98	74	59
4000	2109	1249	884	683	556	469	406	357	319	289	195	147	118	99	74	59
5000	2254	1294	905	696	565	475	410	361	322	291	196	148	118	99	74	60
6000	2358	1326	920	704	570	479	413	363	324	292	196	148	119	99	74	60
7000	2437	1348	931	710	574	482	415	365	325	293	197	148	119	99	74	60
8000	2499	1366	939	715	577	484	417	366	326	294	197	148	119	99	75	60
9000	2548	1380	945	719	580	486	418	367	327	295	198	149	119	99	75	60
10000	2589	1391	950	722	582	487	419	368	327	295	198	149	119	99	75	60
15000	2716	1426	966	731	587	491	422	370	329	297	198	149	119	100	75	60
20000	2782	1443	974	735	590	493	423	371	330	297	199	149	119	100	75	60
25000	2823	1454	979	738	592	494	424	372	331	298	199	149	120	100	75	60
30000	2851	1461	982	740	593	495	425	372	331	298	199	149	120	100	75	60
35000	2871	1466	984	741	594	496	425	372	331	298	199	149	120	100	75	60
40000	2886	1470	986	742	595	496	426	373	331	298	199	150	120	100	75	60
45000	2898	1473	988	743	595	497	426	373	332	299	199	150	120	100	75	60
50000	2908	1476	989	743	596	497	426	373	332	299	199	150	120	100	75	60

Table E.4a. Probabilities of including at least one occurrence in a sample (discovery sampling)

Probability level 99%
Sample size when occurrence rate is

Field size	0.1	0.2	0.3	0.4	0.5	0.6	0.7	0.8	0.9	1.0	1.5	2.0	2.5	3.0	4.0	5.0
200	200	200	200	199	198	196	193	189	185	180	157	137	120	107	88	74
300	300	300	298	294	286	277	267	256	246	235	192	161	138	120	96	79
400	400	399	391	378	360	341	323	305	289	274	214	175	148	127	100	82
500	500	495	477	450	421	392	366	342	320	301	229	185	154	132	103	84
600	600	587	554	512	471	433	400	370	344	322	240	191	159	135	105	85
700	699	674	622	565	512	466	427	392	363	337	249	196	162	138	106	86
800	797	755	683	610	547	494	448	410	378	350	255	200	165	140	107	87
900	895	830	737	650	577	516	467	425	390	360	260	203	167	141	108	88
1000	990	900	785	684	602	536	482	438	401	369	264	206	168	142	109	88
1500	1430	1177	961	804	688	601	533	478	434	397	278	213	173	146	111	89
2000	1800	1368	1072	875	738	637	561	500	451	411	285	217	176	148	112	90
2500	2104	1505	1147	923	770	661	578	514	463	421	289	220	178	149	113	90
3000	2354	1608	1202	956	793	677	591	524	470	427	292	222	179	150	113	91
4000	2735	1751	1275	1000	823	698	607	536	480	435	296	224	180	151	113	91
5000	3009	1845	1322	1028	841	712	616	544	486	440	298	225	181	151	114	91
6000	3215	1912	1354	1048	854	720	623	549	490	443	299	226	181	152	114	91
7000	3374	1962	1378	1062	863	727	628	553	493	446	300	227	182	152	114	92
8000	3501	2001	1397	1072	870	732	632	555	496	448	301	227	182	152	114	92
9000	3605	2032	1411	1081	875	736	634	558	497	449	302	227	182	152	114	92
10000	3690	2057	1423	1087	880	739	637	559	499	450	302	228	183	152	114	92
15000	3965	2135	1459	1108	893	748	644	565	503	454	304	229	183	153	115	92
20000	4113	2175	1478	1119	900	753	647	567	505	455	305	229	183	153	115	92
25000	4206	2200	1489	1125	904	756	649	569	506	456	305	229	184	153	115	92
30000	4269	2216	1496	1129	907	758	651	570	507	457	305	229	184	153	115	92
35000	4315	2228	1502	1133	909	759	652	571	508	458	306	230	184	153	115	92
40000	4350	2238	1506	1135	911	760	653	572	508	458	306	230	184	153	115	92
45000	4377	2245	1509	1137	912	761	653	572	509	458	306	230	184	153	115	92
50000	4399	2250	1512	1138	913	762	654	572	509	458	306	230	184	153	115	92

Bibliography

ANSI/ASQC A-3 1987. *Quality Systems Terminology*. Milwaukee, Wisc.: ASQC, 1987.

ANSI/ASQC MI-1987. *American National Standard for Calibration Systems*. Milwaukee, Wisc.: ASQC, 1987.

ANSI/ISO/ASQC Q9001-1994. *Quality Systems—Model for Quality Assurance in Design/Development, Production, Installation and Servicing*. Milwaukee, Wisc.: ASQC, 1994.

ANSI/ISO/ASQC Q9004-1-1994. *Quality Management and Quality System Elements—Guidelines*. Milwaukee, Wisc.: ASQC, 1994.

ANSI/ASQC Q1-1986. *Generic Guidelines for Auditing of Quality Systems*. Milwaukee, Wisc.: ASQC, 1986.

ANSI/ISO/ASQC Q10011-1-1994. *Guidelines for Auditing Quality Systems*. Milwaukee, Wisc.: ASQC, 1994.

ANSI/ISO/ASQC Q10011-2-1994. *Guidelines for Auditing Quality Systems—Qualification Criteria for Quality Systems Auditors*. Milwaukee, Wisc.: ASQC, 1994

ANSI/ASME N45.2-1977. *QA Program Requirements for Nuclear Facilities*. New York: ASME, 1977.

Arkin, Herbert. *Handbook of Sampling for Auditing and Accounting*. 3d ed. Englewood Cliffs, N.J.: Prentice Hall, 1984.

Arter, Dennis R. *Quality Audits for Improved Performance*. 2d ed. Milwaukee, Wisc.: ASQC Quality Press, 1994.

ASME NQA-1C-1992. *Quality Assurance Program Requirements for Nuclear Facilities*. New York: ASME, 1992.

ASQC. Auditor Certification booklet. Milwaukee, Wisc.: ASQC, 1994.

ASQC Education and Training Committee of the Energy Division. *Quality Systems Auditor Training Handbook*. 2d ed. Milwaukee, Wisc.: ASQC, 1986.

ASQC Quality Audit Technical Committee. Edited by Charles B. Robinson. *How to Plan an Audit*. Milwaukee, Wisc.: ASQC, 1987.

ASQC Quality Cost Committee. Edited by John Campanella. *Principles of Quality Costs*. 2d ed. Milwaukee, Wisc.: ASQC Quality Press, 1990.

Bethlehem Steel Corporation. QA *Subcommittee and Purchasing, Supplier Excellence Training Program*. Bethlehem, Penn.: Bethlehem Steel Corporation, 1991.

Bossert, James. *Procurement Quality Control*. 4th ed. Milwaukee, Wisc.: ASQC Quality Press, 1988.

Cheaney, Lee, and Maury Cotter. *Real People, Real Work, Parables on Leadership in the '90s*. 2d ed. Knoxville, Tenn.: SPC Press, 1991.

Deming, W. Edwards. *Out of the Crisis*. Cambridge, Mass.: MIT Center for Advanced Engineering Study, 1986

Department of Defense. *H.Q.U.S.A.F./RDCM, MIL-Q-9858A*. Washington, D.C., 1965.

Department of Defense. *AMCQA, H-50 Handbook*. Washington, D.C., 1965.

Department of Defense. *ARMY-MI, MIL-STD-45662A*. Washington, D.C., 1988.

Feigenbaum, Armand V. *Total Quality Control*. 3d ed. New York: McGraw-Hill, 1983.

Fisher, Edward S. *Auditor Workshop*. Greensburg, Penn.: Eagles International, 1990.

GOAL/QPC. *The Memory Jogger*. 2d ed. Metheun, Mass.: GOAL/QPC, 1988.

Gitlow, Howard, Shelly Gitlow, Alan Oppenheim, and Rosa Oppenheim. *Tools and Methods for the Improvement of Quality*. Homewood, Ill. and Boston: Richard D. Irwin, 1989.

Grant, Eugene L. and Richard S. Leavenworth. *Statistical Quality Control*. 5th ed. New York: McGraw-Hill, 1980.

Hutchins, Greg. *Standard Manual of Quality Auditing*. Englewood Cliffs, N.J.: Prentice Hall, 1992.

Interstate Commerce Commission. *Table of 105,100 Random Decimal Digits*. Washington, D.C.: Bureau of Transportation, Economics, and Statistics, 1982.

ISO 8402. *Quality—Vocabulary*. Geneva: International Standards Organization, 1987.

Johnson, Ross H., and Richard T. Weber. *Buying Quality*. Milwaukee, Wisc.: ASQC Quality Press, 1988.

Johnson, L. Marvin. *Quality Assurance Program Evaluation*. West Covina, Calif.: L. Marvin Johnson, 1990.

———. *Quality Assurance Evaluator's Workbook*. West Covina, Calif.: L. Marvin Johnson, 1987.

Juran, Joseph M. *Juran's Quality Control Handbook*. 4th ed. New York: McGraw-Hill, 1988.

Lammermeyer, Horst U. *Human Relations—The Key to Quality*. Milwaukee, Wisc.: ASQC Quality Press, 1990.

Nuclear Regulatory Commission. Appendix B of 10 CFR Part 50 in *Quality Assurance Criterion for Nuclear Power Plants*. Washington, D.C.: Federal Register National Archives and Records, 1992.

Professional Standards and Responsibilities Committee. *Standards for the Practice of Internal Auditing*. Altamonte Springs, Fla.: Institute of Internal Auditors, 1978.

Quality Management International. *Quality System Auditor Training Course Manual*. Exton, Penn.: Quality Management International, 1994.

Robinson, Charles B. *Auditing a Quality System for the Defense Industry.* Milwaukee, Wisc.: ASQC Quality Press, 1990.

Sawyer, Lawrence B. *The Practice of Modern Internal Auditing.* 3d ed. Altamonte Springs, Fla.: Institute of Internal Auditors, 1988.

Sayle, Allan J. *Management Audits.* 2d ed. Great Britain: McGraw- Hill, 1988.

Tables of Probability for Use in Exploratory Sampling. Washington, D.C.: Auditor General, U.S. Air Force, 1957.

Thresh, James L. *How to Plan, Conduct and Benefit from Effective Quality Audits.* White Plains, N.Y.: MGI Management Institute, 1984.

Western Electric Technologies. *Statistical Quality Control Handbook.* 11th ed. Indianapolis: Western Electric Technologies, 1985.

Index